WATCHMAN, WATCHMAN, What of the Night?

JOY PARROTT

What Leaders Are Saying

"Joy Parrott's book, <u>Watchman, Watchman What of the Night</u>, is a clear and much needed sounding of God's shofar for all of us. It calls us first to recognize and admit the services of God's watchmen; second, to respond, mainly first by the intercessory prayers to which they call us. As I read Joy's book, chapter by chapter I thought, "What needless casualties of war have beset us, if only we had had this book beforehand and heeded its calls and warnings!" This book is timely – if not tardy – for every leader and budding watchman on the walls

John Loren Sandford
Co-Founder, Elijah House, Inc.

Joy Parrott's book is a "now" word to the body of Christ! The relationship between the leaders and the watchman is desperately needed today! Joy's revelation is replete with scriptures and personal examples to call the leaders and the watchmen to a place of unity and team work so the Kingdom of God can advance, unhindered, in the earth!

Jill Austin
Master Potter Ministries

Spiritual warfare is accelerating in these last days. There is a great conflict of good and evil going on that will only increase. When watchmen and intercessors work together with leaders, we will see ultimate victory over the powers of darkness. The information in this book, if applied, can prevent you from becoming a casualty, and that is why I highly recommend it.

Kari Browning
Apostolic Team, The Gateway Christian Fellowship

Let's get honest here! Joy Parrott's first book, **PARABLES IN THE NIGHT SEASONS** remains one of our all-time best sellers here at THE ELIJAH LIST (We've sold <u>THOUSANDS OF COPIES</u> --just so you know) now **WATCHMAN, WATCHMAN, WHAT OF THE NIGHT?** demonstrates that just as dreams are crucial to the Church, so too are the Watchmen (man or woman) --because as Joy says in the book, "Watchmen" are to 'guard, to protect, to peer into the distance, to spy, to scope something out---**especially in order to 'see' and 'to warn those who are in danger.'**" Now how can you, or anyone in the Church resist the revelation in this book?

Steve Shultz
THE ELIJAH LIST
www.elijahlist.com

WATCHMAN, WATCHMAN
What of the Night?

JOY PARROTT

GLORY PUBLICATIONS

Acknowledgements

My thanks and gratitude to all of the following people...

- Jesse Parrott, my husband, who has walked through the challenges of being married to a watchman. And what challenges those are--from the endless listening of dreams, by allowing me to process, to having to pick me up off the floor when the revelation was not received. I thank you. Your support has meant a lot to me. I love you!

- To Jameson, Jonathan and Janaya, my beautiful children who are also called as watchmen on the wall! Thank you for lending your mother to the work of the Lord and thank you for sharing your dreams and discernment in different matters. Although you may not have understood the things you were sharing, God used you to help bring revelation to many situations. I love you all!

- Linda Blaylock, my ministry assistant, who has encouraged and uplifted me throughout the years. Your support and prayers have kept me pursuing all that God has required of me. Thank you for your consistent love and support even through difficult times. You are loved!

- Kari Browning, who continuously reminds me how much the body of Christ needs this teaching! Your support has brought healing in my life and as a result of this book, will hopefully bring healing to many who have walked in the difficult task of being a watchman. I appreciate you.

- Greg Wilkinson, who took on the challenge of editing my work once again. If it wasn't for your gifts and willingness to clean up the manuscript, we wouldn't have a book to read. Thank you. I appreciate you and all your help.

- To my personal intercessors and watchmen, I can't thank you enough for standing in the gap and taking the hits for me. Thank you for remaining on the wall and pressing through! May God reward you for your diligence in prayer and give refreshing for those middle-of-the-night prayer times!

- To the leaders that God put in my life for the training of the role as watchman, I thank you. Although you may not have agreed with the revelation I brought, God used you to help develop this gifting as watchman, which ultimately resulted in the teachings of this book.

- Finally and most importantly, my Heavenly Father who is my best friend, counselor, encourager and comforter. This is His book and to Him I give all the glory, honor and praise!

Table of Contents

Foreword

In your hands is a comprehensive tool to help ground and guide today's growing army of worshipful watchers and watching intercessors. In composing the foreword for this manuscript, let me first start out by mentioning the excellence of character of the author. This is not just another book. This is a major part of Joy Parrott's lifestyle. She lives the message that is enclosed in these pages. Joy is a watchman with a heart for God purposes for the body of Christ, congregations both small and large and for whole cities to be touched by the transforming nature and power of Christ.

Having been an intercessor now for over three decades, I can smell when it is just "good shop talk" and when the person has actually been in the trenches doing the stuff. Add this manuscript to Dutch Sheets' Watchman Prayer and my book Kneeling on the Promises and you will have a three-cord strand that will not quickly be torn a part!

Learn lessons about the role of the watchman, how to handle "discernment" and yet keep your spirit free from offense. Learn how to exercise Christ authority in your sphere of influence; strengthen your foundation and how to mature as a watchman. Go on a journey and gain wisdom on how to walk honorably with leaders, avoid charismatic witchcraft and staying within your boundaries!

The contents of this book might just save your neck from a heap of a lot of trouble! "Wow – this book should have been written a long time ago", I think I can hear some of you saying! Well, it is written now and it is right where it belongs – right in your hands! But now, like the author, read the word, meditate on the word and become the contents that are written.

This book will add needed wisdom for any serious minded person who loves God with all their heart and want to see His Kingdom come to their city. With gladness of heart, I commend to you the writings of Joy Parrott on the watchman anointing.

James W. Goll
Cofounder of Encounters Network – a ministry to the nations
Author of The Seer, The Lost Art of Intercession, Praying for Israel's Destiny, Kneeling on the Promises and a host of others!

Preface

This book was commissioned by God while writing my first book, *Parables in the Night Seasons; Understanding Your Dreams.* One night during the writing of *"Parables,"* God gave me a dream in which I was told to write another book. Upon waking, I was not happy to realize that another book was on its way since I had just begun the first. At the time, I had been rather intimidated about writing a book, so to think that I would be writing another did not bring rejoicing! However, I did ask God what the name of the book would be, to which He responded, *Watchman, Watchman, What of the Night?* The title relieved me since it was a topic that I was very familiar with. I then submitted to God about writing the book, but not without negotiations! I asked God if I could first wait until the publishing of the first book. I wanted to see how the whole book process went so that I would be familiar with it the second time around. God was gracious and granted my request. Since the publishing of *Parables*, I have been reminded not only by God, but also by many of my readers that they are waiting for *Watchman, Watchman, What of the Night?*

One of the challenges that I found while trying to learn the role of a watchman was that there weren't a lot of books on this subject. For that reason, I was quickly enrolled in the "School of Hard Knocks" and my teacher's name was Holy Spirit! During my years of attending this school, a few books began to appear on the watchman. However, these books were devoted more to the watch of a city, region or nation and did not give much attention to the watch of the local body.

As a watchman for the body of Christ, I have recognized the need for teaching in this specific area. It is my desire in *Watchman, Watchman, What of the Night?* to bring forth the much needed revelation that God has imparted to me. I realize that there are many that function in the watchman role and there can be many different spheres of anointing and authority. However, I will be devoting much of my teaching to the area of the watchman within the local church. I hope to impart healing and instruction to both the watchman and to the leaders. In my travels, I have seen many a wounded warrior, both in the watchman and their leaders because of the lack of understanding concerning the role of watchman. I believe this is the hour for the teaching and revelation to come forth, and I also believe it is the will of the Father that the leaders and watchmen flow together like peanut butter and jelly, salt and pepper, tick and tock. I pray that many will be healed, instructed and set in their role to function the way God has intended them.

Unlike my first book, I have purposefully withheld writing a lot of personal stories in order to keep from exposing anyone and bringing additional hurt or wounding. I thank God for the training He gave me through the difficult situations I encountered and my hope is that the reader will also be equipped through the teachings on the pages to follow.

Chapter One

What is a Watchman?

Imagine living in a time in which there were no televisions, radios, computers, and telephones, radars or any other means of communicating impending dangers. What would it be like? How would we know and communicate about any threats coming our way? I imagine it would be very difficult. We would most likely find out about the danger only as we became victims of it.

Translated in Biblical Terms

In biblical times, people did not have our technological means for the sending and receiving of warnings. So how did they keep their communities alert to attacks? Let's take a look at what their defense may have been.

When the twelve spies returned to Moses to bring their report about the Promised Land, they said in Deuteronomy 1:28:

> *'Where can we go up? Our brethren have discouraged our hearts, saying, "The people are greater and taller than we;* **the cities are great and fortified up to heaven;** *moreover we have seen the sons of the Anakim there."'*

These cities were unlike ours in that they were fortified by having walls surrounding them. These walls were extremely high and wide with different gates and points of entry into the cities. If the spies were claiming these walls were great and fortified up to heaven, then they must have been very tall! These walls were designed to keep enemy forces out. But even strong walls and double gates could not always secure a city from the enemy. Men were employed to watch day and night upon the walls and gates. Well-trained men were positioned to look out beyond the city to see if there were any enemies approaching the city or camp. Not only were these men able to see out beyond the city, they were also able to see what was going on inside the city. These men were called "watchmen."

Watchmen were stationed on the highest part of a city wall to warn inhabitants of an approaching enemy or messenger.

> *Now **a watchman stood on the tower** in Jezreel, and he saw the company of Jehu as he came, and said, "I see a company of men." And Joram said, "Get a horseman and send him to meet them, and let him say, 'Is it peace?'"* (II Kings 9:17).

> **Set up the standard on the walls** *of Babylon;* **Make the guard strong, set up watchmen,** *prepare the ambushes. For the Lord has both devised and done what He spoke against the inhabitants of Babylon* (Jeremiah 51:12).

> *Now David was sitting between the two gates.* **And the watchman went up to the roof over the gate to the wall,** *lifted his eyes and looked, and there was a man running alone* (II Samuel 18:24).

Now I want you to imagine with me that you are one of the inhabitants in these cities going about your business. How far would you be able to see if you were to look beyond the city walls? My guess is that you would not see much off in the distance. It would be unlikely for you to know if there was any impending danger approaching. Your first clue might be as you were rudely interrupted in your daily schedule to a loud barrage of noise and clamoring about to some damage already present or just occurring.

Now imagine with me that you are on top of one of these high walls in the city. It is very likely that you can see a pretty good distance out from the city upon this high wall. You would now be in a position to see if there was any approaching danger or attack coming. And you would possibly have time to do something about the situation. You would likely have enough time to prepare yourself for the attack, run and hide or do something! Even if you were able to save yourself, what could you do to help those innocent bystanders that are wandering about doing their everyday tasks in the city?

The height of these walls made it easier for the guards upon the wall to see far. As we were just imagining, if you were to stand from inside the city at the base of the wall and peer out, you wouldn't see very far into the distance, but the higher you are the farther you see. Thus, upon the wall the watchmen were able to see potential danger approaching **long before it reached the city.** If they saw something suspicious, they needed to warn the king so the city could be prepared for an attack. The watchmen were to keep careful watch and report of any impending danger to the city before a surprise attack arrived. This would give those in the city time to prepare in order to fight against the attack and possibly save the city from destruction. This is why the watchmen were so necessary. Watchmen became the only source of communicating impending danger to their communities. Thus, watchmen were like the telephones, radios, television and radar of our day.

Spiritual Watchmen

If we were to look at the spiritual significance of this picture, we would see the importance for the need of the spiritual watchman. We have need for them to take their place upon the walls of our cities. Not just our cities, but we also need watchmen over our individual homes, churches, regions, states, countries and beyond.

God has given us a way to communicate impending danger in the spirit realm and that is through the spiritual watchmen. Because it is my desire to instruct the watchman over the local church body, I will concentrate on the role of the watchman within the church or local ministry.

Let's just say the city represents the church. God has given us a way to communicate an attack of the enemy against the church. He has given us spiritual watchmen. They have been stationed in the Spirit upon the high walls and have the ability to see approaching danger, long before it hits the church. Not only can they see the dangers approaching from outside the church, but also God has given them the ability to see inside the church and the problems that may be found there.

Some of the Hebrew meanings for the word "watchman" are "to guard, to protect, maintain, observe and preserve." In another sense, it can mean to lean forward, i.e. "to peer into the distance, to spy, deep watch, to scope something out," especially in order to see approaching danger, and to warn those who are in danger. It is translated "a king's guard, those who look out from a tower in the city wall." It can also be "a sentry, a guard, a soldier stationed to prevent unauthorized passage." The spiritual meaning is watchman or prophets who look out, see danger and report to the people.

> *"Son of man, I have made you a watchman for the house of Israel; therefore hear a word from My mouth, and give them warning from Me"* (Ezekiel 3:17).

From the understanding of these meanings, we can see why God may anoint some to be watchmen over the work He has entrusted to man. While the leader of the church is busy doing the work God has called him to do, the watchman is positioned to see any approaching danger so that the work will not be destroyed. Unfortunately, the church has not operated very well in this capacity.

Below you will find an excerpt from an article written by Rick Joyner entitled, *"The Perfect Storms"* under the subtitle *"Watchman to Your Stations"*:

> *"The watchmen on the walls are those who have an elevated place of both vision and protection.*

They can see either the enemy or the Lord coming from a distance. It was their job to communicate to the elders who sat in the gates what they were seeing so that the elders could determine how to respond. Of course, if it was the king or his representative, the elder would command the gates to be opened and sound the alarm that would begin the proper protocol for welcoming them. If the ones approaching were deemed to be a threat, the elder would then close the gate and sound the alarm to mobilize the forces protecting the city. **Every congregation and city needs these spiritual watchmen in their places at this time. Those who do not have them will be victims of what could have otherwise been prevented.**"

"Today's counterpart to the watchmen who walked about the streets of the city are those who are called to move about the body of Christ **watching for problems that are arising from within. They not only guard against robbers and thieves which have somehow gained entry into the church, but also will be the first to spot fires or other dangers.**" [1]

I also like what Dutch Sheets had to say in his book entitled Watchman Prayer. This is one of the best books that I have read on the watchman. He states:

"The watchmen on the wall also looked for enemies. When they saw potential danger approaching, they sounded an alarm either by a shout or with a trumpet blast. Soldiers could then prepare themselves for battle and defend the city. Watchmen do this today, in a spiritual sense. They alert the Body of Christ to attacks of the enemy, sounding the alarm. **When the**

*watchmen are functioning properly, we need never
be caught off guard by Satan and his forces.* This
may seem somewhat idealistic, but I'm convinced of
its truth. I don't believe God ever intends for Satan
to 'take advantage' or get the bigger portion (see
2 Cor. 2:11). The famed Dutch evangelist Corrie
ten Boom was right to observe: 'It's a poor soldier
indeed who does not recognize the enemy.' The key
to victory in both natural and spiritual warfare is
to clearly identify the enemy, and to understand his
character and methods."* [2]

I like what Dutch says, "When the watchmen are functioning
properly, we need never be caught off guard by Satan and his forces."
Jesus did not have victory over the enemy so that we could lose the
battle to Satan.

*"Lest Satan should take advantage of us; for we are
not ignorant of his devices."* (II Corinthians 2:11).

God does not want us to be ignorant of Satan's devices. We need
to understand that our enemy is real and he has devised plans to try
to take down our ministries. We should not be unaware of these
schemes. God will expose the tactics of the enemy through our
watchmen. By employing the watchmen, we can spare ourselves
much defeat in regards to our ministries.

*"Be sober, be vigilant; because your adversary the
devil walks about like a roaring lion, seeking whom
he may devour"* (I Peter 5:8).

God will alert us to our adversary and his plans if we will allow
the watchmen to function in the role God has called them to. Without
the watchmen on the walls, we will fall prey to the enemy's schemes
and have undue disaster or tragedies.

In my book, *Parables in the Night Seasons: Understanding Your*

Dreams, I wrote about an object lesson God had given me showing the importance of the role of the watchman. Let me reiterate it here.

At the time of this lesson, I did not have an anti-virus protection program on my computer. Consequently, a virus infected the computer. Unaware of this, an attachment, which spread the virus, was sent to the people in my address book and continued to spread the virus. Some of the recipients had a virus protection program and fortunately were warned concerning it. If my computer had this program, it would have alerted me to this problem and could have spared me the results of infected files.

I learned a valuable lesson through this process. We all have need of a watchman in our lives. They are able to see the blind spots that we are unable to see. Many problems could be avoided if, like the virus protection program, we were alerted to the potential danger the enemy has sent our way.

I have a few other passages from the book Watchman Prayer that I would like to insert here. Dutch Sheets says:

> *"God helps watchmen by pointing out what needs to be seen and heard **to aid the growth and health of a church.**"*

> *"There are people who come into churches or ministries with impure motives. **If not discovered soon enough, they can do great damage. The anointing of the watchman will detect them,** and they can either be exposed or neutralized in prayer so that they are unable to create problems."* [3]

This is just like having a virus protection program on your computer. The watchmen aid in the growth and health of a church. They are able to detect those with impure motives that could possibly cause a cancer to grow within the body. It is time for us to get our spiritual anti-virus protection program in place. This can only happen by installing our watchmen onto the walls of our ministries!

In the next chapter we will further explore what God has to say concerning the watchman.

---

[1] Rick Joyner, The Perfect Storms, *The Morning Star Prophetic Bulletin,* March 2003. Used by permission. www.morningstarministries.org

[2] Dutch Sheets, *Watchman Prayer* (Ventura, CA: Regal Books, 2000), p. 36.

[3] Sheets, *Watchman Prayer,* pp. 66-67.

Chapter Two

The Role of a Watchman

In the previous chapter we caught a glimpse of what a watchman does and set the stage for a further look into the role of a watchman. Although we do not have watchmen set upon the walls of our cities today, we do have police and security guards roaming the streets of our cities. We also have state patrol that work outside the city limits. And we have our military police and security for the protection of our government. These trained men and women are employed to uphold the law and keep innocent people from harm as best as can be done. They are probably the closest example we have in the natural to what the biblical times had as a physical watchman. So what about the spiritual watchman? Since we want to relate the spiritual significance of a watchman, we need to turn to the Word of God.

What God Says

A good example to look at from the Scriptures on a spiritual watchman would be found in Ezekiel. God speaks to Ezekiel on more than one occasion about how the watchman role is to work. Let's take a look.

> *Now it came to pass at the end of seven days that the word of the Lord came to me, saying, "Son of man, I have made you a watchman for the house of Israel; therefore hear a word from My mouth, and give them warning from Me"* (Ezekiel 3:16,17).

"So you, son of man: I have made you a watchman for the house of Israel; therefore you shall hear a word from My mouth and warn them for Me" (Ezekiel 33:7).

There are two things that we can glean from these scriptures. The first thing we need to see is that God made Ezekiel a watchman. Man did not choose him. The leaders did not choose him. The military did not choose him. God chose him. Watchmen can be trained but God is the one who does the choosing, commissioning and calling for this position.

I rather doubt that Ezekiel volunteered to be a watchman for the house of Israel. You don't have to get very far into the book of Ezekiel to see that his job of watchman was not a pleasant one! God made Ezekiel to be a sign to the house of Israel for their disobedience and he required Ezekiel to walk out some rather strange things. Ezekiel uses prophecies, parables, signs and symbols to dramatize God's message concerning the rebellion of the children of Israel. Ezekiel was called to speak about the coming judgment and captivity the Israelites were going to face. I'm sure that did not make him a very popular person. The people must have thought Ezekiel to be a crazy man. I know that we would be calling for the straight jacket if we saw a man outside, confined to lie on his side for over a year, cooking his rationed food over cow manure and prophesying against us (see Ezekiel 4:4-32). I can't imagine anyone in his right mind volunteering for this job.

The second thing we need to see from these scriptures is that Ezekiel as a watchman was to hear a word from God and give the people warning **from God**. Ezekiel did not speak on his own accord but on God's. The warning was coming from God, not from Ezekiel. Ezekiel was only the messenger. Yet, Ezekiel had a great responsibility to give this warning.

"When I say to the wicked, 'O wicked man, you shall surely die!' and you do not speak to warn the wicked from his way, that wicked man shall die in his

iniquity; but his blood I will require at your hand. Nevertheless if you warn the wicked to turn from his way, and he does not turn from his way, he shall die in his iniquity; but you have delivered your soul" (Ezekiel 33:8-9).

This scripture passage would put the fear of the Lord into any watchman. If Ezekiel did not give the warning, he would be held responsible for the blood of all those who perished for lack of being warned. The only way that Ezekiel would not be found guilty for the blood of the people is by giving the word of warning. By giving the warning it guaranteed that Ezekiel would not be found responsible for the death of others.

God never desires to see the wicked die in their way. He desires to see them turn, repent and live.

"Do I have any pleasure at all that the wicked should die?" says the Lord God, "and not that he should turn from his ways and live?" (Ezekiel 18:23).

"For I have no pleasure in the death of one who dies," says the Lord God. "Therefore turn and live!" (Ezekiel 18:32).

"Say to them; 'As I live,' says the Lord God, 'I have no pleasure in the death of the wicked, but that the wicked turn from his way and live. Turn, turn from your evil ways! For why should you die, O house of Israel?'" (Ezekiel 33:11).

God is a just God and fair in all He does. He is not up in heaven with a big stick just waiting for us to mess up so that He can send His wrath upon us. He grieves at the idea of having to pour out judgment. He would rather we repent and turn so that He could relent. Because He is a God of justice, He requires judgment for sin. However, because of His great mercies, He gives us time to repent and turn from going the wrong way. He doesn't want to see the fall of man. This is why He gave His only son to die for us, so that we might live. Yet, at the same time, He gave us a free will and He will not interfere with our free will. When we choose to continue in sin, we must suffer the consequences of our actions. There is the law of sowing and reaping and we cannot escape it. Even in all this, God will still warn us before trouble should come.

One might say that we don't have need of the watchman to come and warn us any longer. We live in a time of grace. We have the Holy Spirit residing within us and He will warn us directly. It is true that we live in a time of His great grace. Unlike those in the Old Testament, we have His Holy Spirit and have the ability to hear directly from Him. Yet, we do not always see our blind spots so God still needs to give us watchmen to help us.

In the last chapter we spoke of the spiritual symbolism of the city representing the church. Therefore we would have to consider the king to symbolize the leader. The leader has been commissioned to train, disciple and equip the body of Christ. Any one of the five-fold ministry has this responsibility (see Ephesians 4:11,12). While the leaders are busy doing what God has called them to do, they cannot always see the attack of the enemy in regards to the work God has given them. Because of this, He still gives the gift of watchman to the body of Christ.

Among other things, the Apostle Paul was a watchman.

> *"For I have not shunned to declare to you the whole counsel of God. Therefore take heed to yourselves and to all the flock, among which the Holy Spirit has made you overseers, to shepherd the church of God which He purchased with His own blood. For I know this, that after my departure savage wolves will come in among you, not sparing the flock. Also from among yourselves men will rise up, speaking perverse things, to draw away the disciples after themselves. Therefore watch, and remember that for three years I did not cease to warn everyone night*

and day with tears" (Acts 20:27-31).

Basically, this scripture is saying that Paul warned the leaders and overseers for three years. As a watchman on the wall, Paul was able to see the enemy before he made his way into the camp. He talks about the enemy being like wolves coming in among them. We can also see from this passage that not only did he see the enemy approaching the camp, but also he saw what was going on inside the camp when he declares, *"Also from among yourselves men will rise up, speaking perverse things, to draw the disciples after them."* Now if this was obvious for them to see, then they would not have needed Paul to warn them for over a period of three years. Paul was sure that when he was gone these things would happen because they had already been revealed to him, as a watchman, he gave the warning.

These things are still happening in the church today. We have the "wolves" sent in to the church by the enemy, and we have those amongst us whom are speaking perverse things and drawing the disciples after them. Paul exhorts the leaders to watch and remember the warnings.

From this passage I can see that as a watchman, Paul wept over the thought of the enemy being able to come in and destroy the work of the Lord. We also should weep over this. We need to take seriously the warnings that God gives us. We have an enemy and he wants to destroy our families, our churches and our ministries. He will not stop at anything to have victory in this area. The scripture warns us to stay alert to him.

> *"Be sober, be vigilant, because your adversary the devil walks about like a roaring lion seeking whom he may devour"* (1Peter 5:8).

> *"Lest Satan should take advantage of us; for we are not ignorant of his devices"* (2Corinthians 2:11).

We are not to be ignorant of Satan's devices. Thus, God anointed watchmen to be on the lookout and to see where the enemy may try to devour us. We must heed the warning Paul has given us and shepherd the ministry of God, being watchful lest Satan take advantage of us and the work that God has given us be destroyed.

Careful Instruction

When the watchmen were upon the wall looking out, alert to any approaching danger, they had to be very careful to know when to report to the king. Reporting to the king was given in order to prepare the city for an attack so they had to be very sure that what they were reporting was a real concern to the city. If they reported just anything without being sure that it was danger to the city, it would be like the boy who cried wolf for no reason. As a result, nobody paid attention to the boy when there really was a wolf.

We can have a lot of brush fires and spend all our time putting them out and miss the real fire, or even worse, not be taken seriously when the real fire alarm is sounding. This is exactly what the enemy would have us do. He would love to get us distracted on something less important so that we would not be available for the important issues. He would also love nothing more than to have us appear less credible before others because we cried wolf when we shouldn't have. Therefore, as watchmen we must be able to discern and report only the real dangers.

S o how can we be sure that we do not get hung up on brush fires? How do we know what is of major concern and what is not? How can we know when we are to give a warning? The following scripture reference may bring some answers to these questions.

> *For thus has the Lord said to me: "Go set a watchman, let him declare what he sees." And he saw a chariot with a pair of horsemen, a chariot of donkeys, and a chariot of camels, and he listened earnestly with great care. Then he cried, "A lion, my Lord! I stand continually on the watchtower in the daytime; I have sat at my post every night. And look, here comes a chariot of men with a pair of horsemen!" Then he answered and said, "Babylon is fallen, is fallen! And*

all the carved images of her gods he has broken to the ground." Oh, my threshing and the grain of my floor! That which I have heard from the Lord of hosts, the God of Israel, I have declared to you (Isaiah 21:6-10).

Let's examine these scriptures more closely. There is great revelation we can glean from in this scripture passage. Verse six says,

> For **thus has the Lord said** to me: **"Go, set a watchman, let him declare what he sees."**

This verse starts out with God instructing the people. He tells them to set a watchman upon the wall. God is still instructing us to get our watchmen on the walls. We need to realize that God gave the watchmen to the body of Christ as a gift to them for their protection. We need to recognize that a "watchman" is a critical part of the functioning of the body of Christ. We must set our watchmen into their positions.

He continues to instruct them to allow the watchman to declare what he sees. We also must allow the watchmen to declare that which the Lord is showing them. As I pointed out earlier, the watchman has a very great responsibility before God to declare the warnings, otherwise the watchman will be held responsible for the blood of those he did not warn. Let's continue on with verse seven.

> *And he saw a chariot with a pair of horsemen, a chariot of donkeys, and a chariot of camels, and* ***he listened earnestly with great care***.

In this verse we are reading what the watchman is seeing while upon the wall. He sees chariots and horsemen coming toward the city. Note that "*he listened earnestly with great care*." One of the most important things that a watchman must do when he is shown something from the Lord, is listen earnestly with great care as to what the Lord is saying. Before we can report any warnings, we must know what we are reporting. This is where we determine whether we are dealing with a brush fire or whether we have a real concern on our hands.

Watchmen may be given their revelations in many different forms. Just as God spoke to Ezekiel through prophecies, parables, signs and symbols, He will do the same for the watchmen today. Often watchmen will receive their warnings through dreams and visions. Because many of the ways God chooses to give revelation are parabolic, we must press into the Lord to hear what He is saying. We need understanding and wisdom. Therefore, a watchman should not be quick to rush a word of warning to anyone without being sure of what they have heard or seen. (I cannot emphasize this enough.) If we want to be responsible in our role of watchman then, we must listen earnestly with great care as to what God is saying. It is only after understanding what we are seeing that we should report any warnings. Verse eight says,

> **Then he cried**, *"A lion, my Lord! I stand continually on the watchtower in the daytime; I have sat at my post every night."*

Now he cries, *"A lion, my Lord!"* He first sees, and then listens and inquires of the Lord. Now he understands that this is the enemy. *"A lion, my Lord!"* Our enemy roams about like a roaring lion, seeking whom he may devour. The watchman has declared that he has been at his post both day and night continually watching, alert to any danger. Now he has something to report, so he declares what he has seen and heard. Verse nine says,

> *"**And look**, here comes a chariot of men with a pair of horsemen!"*

I would imagine that as a watchman who stands at his post regularly, that this scene would be rather common. Chariots and horsemen were likely coming through the territory often. What made this situation different? It was what he heard when he listened with great care that made the difference.

I want to point out here that many times watchmen will see something and for the most part many people would not be alerted to the situation or circumstance because it is familiar to them. Yet, well-trained watchmen will sense an alert and the potential danger that it presents. Sometimes without even knowing why, an alarm will go off inside them causing alert to what would look like a rather normal situation or circumstance. I will be presenting more about this aspect of the watchman in chapter three. Let's continue on with verse ten.

> *Oh, my threshing and the grain of my floor!* **That which I have heard from the Lord** *of hosts, the God of Israel,* **I have declared to you.**

In this verse, the watchman is revealing the source of his information. He had listened earnestly and heard from the Lord, and now it was time to declare the warning. Because of his responsibility before God as a watchman, he was releasing his warning and making sure that he was not held accountable for any blood. Once he declared to the people what he saw, he now released himself from any responsibility in regards to the warning.

> *"Son of man, speak to the children of your people and say to them: 'When I bring the sword upon a land and the people of the land take a man from their territory and make him their watchman, when he sees the sword coming upon the land, if he blows the trumpet and warns the people then whoever hears the sound of the trumpet and does not take warning, if the sword comes and takes him away, his blood shall be on his own head.* **He heard the sound of the trumpet, but did not take warning; his blood shall be upon himself. But he who takes warning will save his life'"** (Ezekiel 33:2-5).

Once the warning has been released, it is no longer a concern to the watchman. Now the responsibility lies with those who heard the warning. This does not mean that the watchman does not feel anything. Just as Paul had wept concerning the warnings he had given, watchmen also find themselves weeping over the vile things the enemy has planned against those they love. This should take us into a place of prayer and intercession. (I will cover more on this aspect in later chapters.)

Our prayers as a watchman should be that those to whom the warning has been given would take heed, saving their life, ministry or situation. Many people see a watchman as a bearer of bad news, but that is not what their role was intended to be. God has given the watchman to us because He is trying to spare us of a bad situation or circumstance. The role was given for our protection and preservation. As hard as it is for the watchman to appear to be the bearer of bad news, we should rejoice in knowing that one's life, ministry or situation may be spared as a result of being obedient.

Although we see repeatedly in scripture that the children of Israel did not heed the warnings given and as a result received the impending consequences, we also can find accounts where the warnings were heeded and lives were spared such as in the book of Jonah.

Jonah was given the task of bringing a difficult word of warning to the people of Nineveh. God commissioned Jonah to cry out against the city because their wickedness had come before God. Jonah didn't want to accept the responsibility that God had given him, so he fled from the presence of the Lord, went to Joppa and jumped on a ship going to Tarshish -- the opposite direction God had told him to go!

As we read in the story of Jonah, that displeased God and so Jonah found himself hurled into the sea and swallowed by a great fish where he spent three days and nights in it's belly. (Not exactly my picture of great hotel accommodations!) After crying out to the Lord in his affliction, the great fish finally vomited Jonah onto dry land. By now, Jonah was ready to heed the voice of the Lord and bring the message of warning that God had given him.

As a result of this warning, the people of Nineveh covered themselves with sackcloth and ashes and repented before God for their wrongdoings. They thought perhaps through prayer, fasting and repenting that God might turn from His fierce anger and keep their lives from perishing. God saw their works and He relented from the disaster that was intended to come against them.

In the case of Jonah, a whole city was spared. As difficult as it was to bring the words of warning, people's lives were spared. Whether you think the people will hear and heed the words of warning or not, they must be given if the Lord has told you to do so.

> *"And you, son of man, do not be afraid of them nor be afraid of their words, though briers and thorns are with you and you dwell among scorpions; do not be afraid of their words or dismayed by their looks, though they are a rebellious house. You shall speak My words to them, whether they hear or whether they refuse, for they are rebellious. But you, son of man, hear what I say to you. Do not be rebellious like that rebellious house; open your mouth and eat what I give you"* (Ezekiel 2:6-8).

We cannot be afraid to bring the words of warning. In this passage, God exhorts Ezekiel to give the warnings whether the Israelites will hear or refuse. He goes on to admonish him not to be rebellious. When we choose not to be obedient to the Lord, we are considered rebellious. Jonah was rebellious when he sidestepped God's commissioning by going to Tarshish instead of Nineveh. In the end, God had his way with Jonah and the outcome of his obedience led the Ninevites into right relationship with God.

We want to be watchmen of obedience and also want to be responsible with what God has given us to do. In the next chapter, we will explore the process and making of a mature, responsible watchman.

Chapter Three

The Developing of a Watchman

In the last chapter, we read how God made Ezekiel a watchman. Although God may call, commission and anoint a person to be a watchman, this does not mean that they have the knowledge, understanding and wisdom to function as one. Time, training and experience must be developed in the watchman.

Let us take a baby as an example. A baby is born into this world with his five senses, yet has no understanding of what those senses are used for. He may see something with his eyes but does not recognize what he sees. He may hear sounds but has no way of understanding them. He may feel touch and knows whether it feels good or bad but does not have a concept of where it is coming from. He may experience different tastes or smells but again, has no comprehension of what they are. It's the same for a watchman. When the anointing is placed on the watchman he becomes aware of the surrounding environment but does not have the understanding, wisdom, knowledge or revelation of what he is experiencing. Therefore, the watchman must be trained and equipped in order to understand the role. If we do not train our watchmen they will remain in an immature stage and will not grow to be a healthy, productive, mature watchman.

I would like to quote another excerpt from Rick Joyner's article published in *The Morning Star Prophetic Bulletin* in March 2003. Again you will find this quote under the article, *"The Perfect Storms"* with the subtitle of *"Watchman to Your Stations"*. He writes:

> *"All of these watchmen had to be trained in their duties, and commissioned by the leaders of the cities, the farmers whose fields they watched, or the leaders of the nation whose borders they patrolled. **Likewise, leaders of congregations, missions, and all other ministries must invest in training and deploying watchmen or they are going to suffer increasing loss and unnecessary tragedies.**"* [1]

How it starts

As stated, a watchman starts to receive discernment but lacks understanding concerning it. Just as in the example of the baby, watchmen can receive their warnings or discernment through any of the five senses. They become attuned to the spiritual environment around them, but have no frame of reference for what they are receiving. Watchmen are often alerted by the Holy Spirit without really understanding why they sense something is wrong. Generally, their spiritual senses are heightened more than the average person. It may start with a sense of uneasiness or something unfamiliar happening through one of their senses.

For example, a watchman may be alerted through the sense of smell. Oftentimes there may be an unusual odor that a demonic spirit is omitting and their spiritual sense of smell is discerning it. Other people may not smell this at all. (This is not about smelling someone's body odor because they neglected to bathe or use deodorant!) Often this is an unfamiliar smell that many people have described as smelling like sulfur. Or it can smell like sickness. When I use to visit my dad in the cancer ward of the veteran's hospital, there was a smell of sickness and death in the halls. There are times when this smell will be present in a situation and I am immediately alerted in my spirit.

Taste is another way a watchman may be alerted by the Holy Spirit. Just as the scripture says, "Taste and see that the Lord is good," the watchman can taste the evil that is present. An unusually gross taste will manifest suddenly in the watchman's mouth for no apparent reason. (And it is not because they had garlic for lunch!)

Again, it is because the Holy Spirit is alerting the watchman and wants him to become aware of his surroundings in the spirit.

God can also alert the watchman through the sense of touch. I know for myself that I have felt strange sensations upon shaking an individual's hand or brushing up against a person. This is not an everyday occurrence, so unless I am attuned in the spirit I may overlook what God is warning me about.

Another way that the Holy Spirit may alert us is through the sense of hearing. He may speak into your hearing a word of warning. You may also hear unusual sounds and even a conversation out of your normal hearing range. I have been in a situation where I was in conversation with a person and somehow by the spirit I was able to hear another conversation a distance away. (It is almost like having one of your ears detached and in another area of the room!)

Sight is another way the Holy Spirit will reveal warnings. This can come in the form of a dream, a vision, or just upon looking at someone. Sight is probably the sense that God uses the most frequently for me as a watchman. I am alerted regularly of impending danger through dreams. Dreams and visions are generally a characteristic that follows the role of a watchman. It stands to reason that God would give the watchman dreams. If you think again upon the literal role of the watchman in biblical times, you will remember that men were employed both night and days to stand upon the wall to look out. It is in the nighttime that the enemy plans many of his attacks. He is familiar with the night because that is what he represents, darkness. Jesus came to expose the works of darkness so God will use dreams in the night seasons to expose the works of darkness.

Because dreams and visions are generally parabolic, it is critical for the watchman to have understanding and wisdom concerning the revelations they are receiving. If you believe you are a watchman and are receiving dreams of warnings, then I would advise you to read my book, *Parables in the Night Seasons: Understanding Your Dreams*. This book will help to give you the tools you need to interpret your dreams.

May I take a moment and give some additional revelation to the watchman concerning dreams? (This information had not really been touched on in the book, *Parables in the Night Seasons; Understanding Your Dreams.)* Since God uses symbols and parables in our dreams, we need to recognize that He is not limited to our circumstances and surroundings in order to give us revelations. God may speak a parable to me through what I see in the night season and I may not be able to relate the dream to anything consistent with my life. I may not recognize the people, surroundings or anything else. Yet God wants me to press in for the understanding because He has a word He wants to speak to me.

In II Samuel chapter 12, God sent Nathan to David with a parable after David had sinned with Bathsheba. Let us look at what Nathan said;

> *Then the Lord sent Nathan to David. And he came to him and said to him: "There were two men in one city, one rich and the other poor. The rich man had exceedingly many flocks and herds. But the poor man had nothing, except one little ewe lamb which he had bought and nourished; and it grew up together with him and with his children. It ate of his own food and drank from his own cup and lay in his bosom; and it was like a daughter to him. And a traveler came to the rich man, who refused to take from his own flock and from his own herd to prepare one for the wayfaring man who had come to him; but he took the poor man's lamb and prepared it for the man who had come to him"* (II Samuel 12:1-4).

From this parable, it would appear that this had nothing to do with David. It turns out though, that God was speaking a word to David about his own situation using another situation. Upon hearing this parable, David became very angry at the man's behavior and said to Nathan, "As the Lord lives, the man who has done this shall surely die!" Later Nathan revealed that David was the man he was talking about in the parable.

Not only can God use a parable from a dream to speak to you, but you can also play the character of another person and their situation in a dream. This happens to me frequently. It either appears that I am actually a different person in the dream, or it can be where it is me playing the part in the dream but the circumstances are someone else's. I do not fully understand why God would do this, but I do know it has been helpful for me when wanting to understand someone else's problems. There is a saying, "Unless you walk a mile in someone's shoes, you cannot really understand them."

When this type of dream started appearing, I thought God was giving me a story line for some screenplay or movie! These types of dreams seem so bizarre. How is it that you can be a different person in a dream? Only actors are accustomed to playing the part of a different character! But God quickly revealed to me that this was Him. He also showed me that people who play the part of another person in a dream are generally watchmen. So, watchman, watchman, what are you seeing in the night seasons?

Not only will God use sight through dreams and visions, but He may also use your natural sight and cause you to see something in the Spirit that could bring a word of warning. I remember being in a worship service one time and while I was worshipping I heard the Lord tell me, "Watchman, open your eyes and look around." As I did this, I scanned the room and my eyes landed on this person and the Lord spoke "Jezebel" to me. I was shocked to hear Him say this. This was one of my first encounters with the spirit of Jezebel. The Lord continued to warn me through different experiences about the spirit operating in this person. He also confirmed this through others. This is one other way that God used my sense of sight to alert me.

A word of warning here. Please do not throw the word "Jezebel" around flippantly. Many people have been hurt from being falsely accused of being a Jezebel. I do not take something like this lightly and I expect God to bring a confirmation of this from the mouth of two or three witnesses.

Immature Watchmen

For the immature watchman, everything appears to be an emergency. Because they have these internal alarms going off and lack understanding, they feel as though the situation must be dealt with immediately. They have not gone before God to "listen earnestly with great care" about what they have seen or felt. As watchmen, we cannot panic. Our apprehension can cause alarm to others. We do not want to bring confusion to others and create an atmosphere of fear. A good example of the immature watchmen vs. the mature watchman can be seen in Numbers Chapter 13. Moses sent twelve men to spy out the land that God was giving them. Ten of the spies came back reporting that indeed the land was good, but it was filled with giants and they reacted in despair and defeat. They brought fear and confusion to everyone around them. Only two of the spies possessed an overcoming attitude and knew that God was bigger than any problem a giant might present.

Even in emergency situations, we must learn to operate out of a place of confidence and trust. We must understand that we serve a mighty God and He is well able to overcome the enemy. Fortunately, you don't see doctors and nurses in an emergency room running around with fear and freaking out about what they are seeing!

Another sign of an immature watchman is being suspicious of everyone. They tend to "see a devil behind every bush." As watchmen, we do not have to go searching for evil. The Holy Spirit is quick to alert us to any impending danger. We do not need to go around drumming up more business! Satan loves to see us focus on him rather than God.

Immature watchmen also discuss their revelations with everyone. This is a form of gossip and should not be. The information God gives a watchman is never to be used for gossip. God entrusts to watchmen information concerning individuals or churches and that information should be treated as top secret from the General Himself! Jesus said in John 15:15,

> *"No longer do I call you servants, for a servant does not know what his master is doing; but I have called you friends, for all things that I heard from My Father I have made known to you."*

Jesus calls us His friend. True friends will not gossip about each other. When God reveals vital information to us, we need to keep that information between God and us until He tells us that we are to report this to our leaders. We also need to have a response like Abraham in Genesis chapter 18. Because the Lord considered Abraham His friend, He revealed to Abraham what He was about to do to Sodom and Gomorrah. Abraham immediately started interceding for God to spare the cities on behalf of the righteous. He asked God if He would spare the cities if fifty righteous could be found. God said He would spare them for fifty. Abraham continued before God petitioning for forty-five, then forty, then thirty, then twenty and one last time he petitioned for the cities to be spared if He should find ten. Unfortunately God could not even find ten righteous ones from those cities but He did spare Lot and his family from the destruction. We also need to intercede in the warning situations God reveals to us.

Immature watchmen can also tend to have a critical and judgmental attitude. Rather than seeing people or circumstances through the redemptive eyes of Jesus, they are quick to stone and crucify someone. They are quick to see the splinter in another person's eye and miss the log that is in their own eye. One of the things that is important for us to remember is that we are all in process. There is not one perfect human being amongst us. The only perfect one who walked among us is now sitting at the right hand of the Father. We are all to be conformed to His image, but this is a process and takes time. We need to show mercy and grace to those around us. Can you imagine what our lives would be like if we would pray for others rather than critiquing and judging one another? I'm certain we would see more growth in each other.

Characteristics of a Mature Watchman

A good watchman will be proven to be a trustworthy person and one who is committed to the church or ministry they are called to. Because of their commitment they will lay their life down for the work of God in the ministry that God has put them. Mature watchmen are loyal to the leadership and submitted to those who have been placed in charge over them. They are responsible in the tasks that are assigned to them. Mature watchmen will also be a people of integrity and are upright in character. They are also team players and communicate well with others. They know their sphere of influence and respond accordingly.

Patience is the mark of a maturing watchman. Rather than operating in fear they faithfully trust God and wait upon Him for confirmations concerning what they have discerned. Maturing watchmen use caution and submit their revelations to the leadership, trusting that God will give the answers to the leadership concerning their revelation.

The most necessary characteristic of a mature watchman is being a person of prayer. They will not use their revelations as a form of gossip but for a reason to pray. They recognize the need to take everything to God in prayer. Their prayers come with the redemptive heart of Jesus and they have the ability to recognize that they are not fighting with flesh and blood but with principalities and powers of darkness. Their confidence is in Jesus. They know that greater is He that is in them than he that is in the world and that no weapon formed against them shall prosper.

Humility is another important characteristic of a mature watchman. Generally these watchmen have been through the purging process and have learned that God alone is the one who establishes their credibility. It is their proven character that will mark their maturity and not how many revelations or the amount of accuracy they have. God given authority is based on a person's character and maturity and they recognize this truth.

Basically, a mature watchman will operate in the opposite spirit of the immature watchman. It's time we begin to teach and train our immature watchmen so that they move into a place of maturity and take their rightful positions on the wall.

---

[1] Rick Joyner, The Perfect Storms, *The Morning Star Prophetic Bulletin,* March 2003.
Used by permission. www.morningstarministries.org

Chapter Four

Maturing in Discernment

In the previous chapter I wrote of ways that a watchman might receive his or her discernment; yet as I pointed out, fledgling watchmen often come to us as babes with need of training. Spiritual sensitivity or discernment is not a sign of maturity. Maturity is measured by what the person does with the revelation.

In regards to discernment, there seem to be two types of people: Those who are naive and have no discernment and those who think they discern everything. Yet there is a balance to discernment and balance is where we want to be.

Two Sides of the Pendulum

On one side of the pendulum, we have those who discern everything evil. They are looking for a demon or problem around every corner. Generally, they also operate in much fear. They use what they believe is their gift of discernment to judge everyone and every situation. Prophetic people as a norm tend to start out seeing the negative. In their immaturity, their response is to judge the person or situation they have just discerned. It is not hard for any of us to see that the bride of Christ has many flaws, but the prophetic types will be eager to point them out for us. Judgment is just another way of saying you are better than someone else or that you would handle a situation better than him or her. A mature person will run to God, pray and seek the redemptive heart of God in a situation.

The other side of this pendulum is the person who discerns

nothing or just neglects to consider it, in fear that they may be judging. Most of us do get some form of discernment. Some have exercised their senses and are accustomed to discerning more than others, but I do believe that God intends for all of us to be discerning. The people who land on this side of the pendulum may be receiving discernment from the Lord but they deny the discernment because they don't want to think anything bad concerning another person. It is good to keep yourself pure from judging each other. However, there are times we must listen to the discernment in order to keep ourselves from deception or making unhealthy alliances. We will now explore both sides of this pendulum.

Discernment vs. Judgment

We will start with the first side of the pendulum, the discerning individual. Because this person's discernment has been heightened, they are quick to sense an alarm in a situation or individual. Once they have been alerted, because of their immaturity they do not know how to handle the situation. Most individuals will operate in fear and mishandle the circumstances surrounding what they discerned.

For some time, I had prayed for the gift of discernment. I didn't exactly know what I was praying for. I would hear stories of people seeing into the spirit and having keen discernment and this appealed to me. Once I became aware that my spiritual senses had been awakened, I did not respond in the proper manner. Because I was now seeing things, it brought a great amount of fear. What I saw, felt or heard would sometimes even paralyze me. I had not yet come to realize that "greater is He that is in me, than he who is in the world." So my first response was fear and urgency.

I also sat in the judgment seat. I looked down on the people that I might have discerned something about. I felt like I was somehow better than others were because I didn't have these problems. In situations where I would discern a problem and have to bring the warning to a leader, I would think that I would be a better leader than they would because I would have handled things differently. God allowed me to walk in this manner for some time. Finally one day He taught me something very important. It was during my normal devotional time when I read from I Samuel chapter 16, which changed my whole focus.

> *But the Spirit of the Lord departed from Saul, and a distressing spirit from the Lord troubled him. And Saul's servants said to him, "Surely, a distressing spirit from God is troubling you. Let our master now command your servants, who are before you to seek out a man who is a skillful player on the harp. And it shall be that he will play it with his hand when the distressing spirit from God is upon you, and you shall be well." So Saul said to his servants, "Provide me now a man who can play well, and bring him to me." Therefore Saul sent messengers to Jesse, and said, "Send me your son David, who is with the sheep." And Jesse took a donkey loaded with bread, a skin of wine, and a young goat, and sent them by his son David to Saul. So David came to Saul and stood before him. And he loved him greatly, and he became his armorbearer. Then Saul sent to Jesse, saying, "Please let David stand before me for he has found favor in my sight." And so it was, whenever the spirit from God was upon Saul, that David would take a harp and play it with his hand. Then Saul would become refreshed and well, and the distressing spirit would depart from him* (I Samuel 16:14-23).

There are a few things I want to share with you that the Lord showed me through these verses. First, Saul's servants recognized, or discerned, that Saul had a distressing spirit. They did not judge him for this but sought help for him.

The next thing God revealed to me was that the distressing spirit was not always present in Saul. Verse twenty-three states that David would play his harp for Saul and the distressing spirit would depart from him. It was at this revelation that I realized there is a need to separate the spirit from the person or the situation.

For we do not wrestle against flesh and blood, but against principalities, against powers, against the rulers of the darkness of this age, against spiritual hosts of wickedness in the heavenly places (Ephesians 6:12).

When we are discerning something, we should not go after the person with our judgments. Anyone of us could fall prey to a distressing spirit. Some battle with these spirits on a daily basis without even knowing what they are fighting against. If they were aware of it, I'm sure they would want to be delivered. It is imperative that we realize that these people are a victim to the enemy. Satan and his cohorts are the ones we fight against. The individuals themselves apart from any distressing spirit are probably wonderful persons. We must extend mercy and grace to them while we war in the Spirit against what is influencing them. We should not judge one another.

For judgment is without mercy to the one who has shown no mercy. Mercy triumphs over judgment (James 2:13).

And above all things have fervent love for one another, for love will cover a multitude of sins (I Peter 4:8).

If we judge others then we ourselves will be judged. We must remember that we are all in process of growing into the image of Christ. Many of us still need healing and deliverance from those things that hold us captive. All of us have had to deal with situations and circumstances in our life that have needed the working power of God to set us free. God looks upon the heart of man. We need to do the same. Let us love one another. Remember it is not the individual we are fighting against, but our adversary the devil.

When we do discern some negative things, the mature thing would be to intercede for the person. Jesus did not come to condemn the world but to save the world. Anyone can pass judgment, but how many are willing to lay down his or her life for someone? Can we lay down our life in love and intercession for the one we want to judge? Can we target their area of need, rather than criticizing them? Can we pray and ask God to supply the very virtue that we see is missing? Prophet Larry Randolph said that God told him that His people don't have faults, they have needs. Let us remember this the next time we are determined to judge an individual.

The Other Side of the Pendulum

The other side of the pendulum is the naïve group. It's almost as if they walk around in an imaginary world. They don't see, or want to see, the potential danger that may be threatening them or a loved one.

God created us to be a discerning people. Think about it. When children are very young they are able to discern when something is wrong. They may not understand what they are discerning, but they are alarmed. Have you ever heard a child say, "I don't like that person?" You ask them why and they say, "I don't know, I just don't." Then being the conditioned people we are, we tell the child that it isn't very nice for them to say such things. So now they feel they are wrong by what they discerned. Their discernment is squelched. Later, to our horror, we find out that the person whom they discerned has molested someone. If we continue to push aside the discernment of our children and make them feel like they are wrong, they will avoid the signs when there is an alarming situation.

This is what happened in my life. When I was young, I would feel certain things about individuals, yet I didn't understand them. I can remember one situation in particular in which my mother disregarded my discernment. She had asked a person to babysit for us. I told her that I didn't like the person and not to let this person baby-sit me. My mother asked me why I felt this way, but because I could not give her a good reason, my discernment was considered invalid. Later, I was molested by this person. I do not blame my mother for this since she, like many of us, had been taught that it isn't nice to think badly about someone without good reason. I have been caught in this very trap with my own children. Since having my spiritual senses awakened, I have paid more attention to what my kids may be discerning. A few of my children are very discerning and once I am alerted to their alarm, I quickly pay attention to what they are saying. They have a proven record that they have been correct in their discernment.

One of the reasons God would want us to be discerning is to keep ourselves from deception or making unhealthy alliances with someone. We have an enemy. He is real and we must be alert to him.

> *Be sober, be vigilant; because your adversary the devil walks about like a roaring lion, seeking whom he may devour* (I Peter 5:8).

Overlooking discernment can cause us many problems. The enemy prowls on those who lack discernment or choose to overlook it. God gives us check marks in our spirits when things are not right. We must not overlook them or we become dull to our spiritual senses and end up with troubles.

In Genesis 27, we see how overlooked discernment results in prevailing deception. This is the story about Jacob and Esau. Their father Isaac was growing old and his eyes were failing. He didn't know the time of his death, but he wanted to be sure that he passed a blessing onto his son Esau before he died. He asked Esau to go hunt some game and then cook him a savory meal so the he could bless his firstborn son. Rebekah Isaac's wife overheard her husband's plan. She wanted her son Jacob to be the one who received the blessing so she devised a plan for Jacob to pretend that he was Esau so that he could receive the blessing. She dressed Jacob in his brothers clothing and took the skin of a goat and put in on Jacob's hands and neck. Esau was a hairy man and Isaac would surely recognize the difference between the brothers. Rebekah prepared the savory food for Jacob to bring to his father. All this was done in order to deceive Isaac. The story continues in the following verses:

> *So he went to his father and said, "My father." And he*

*said, "Here I am. Who are you, my son?" Jacob said
to his father, "I am Esau your firstborn; I have done
just as you told me; please arise, sit and eat of my
game, that your soul may bless me." But Isaac said to
his son, "**How is it that you have found it so quickly,
my son?**" And he said, "Because the Lord your God
brought it to me." Then Isaac said to Jacob, "**Please
come near, that I may feel you, my son, whether you
are really my son Esau or not.**" So Jacob went near
to Isaac his father, and he felt him and said, "**The
voice is Jacob's voice, but the hands are the hands
of Esau.**" And he did not recognize him because his
hands were hairy like his brother Esau's hands; so he
blessed him. Then he said, "**Are you really my son
Esau?**" He said, "I am." He said, "Bring it near
to me, and I will eat of my son's game, so that my
soul may bless you." So he brought it near to him,
and he ate; and he brought him wine, and he drank.
Then his father Isaac said to him, "Come near now
and kiss me, my son." And he came near and kissed
him; and he smelled the smell of his clothing and
blessed him and said: "Surely, the smell of my son is
like the smell of a field which the Lord has blessed.
Therefore may God give you of the dew of heaven,
of the fatness of the earth, and plenty of grain and
wine. Let peoples serve you, and nations bow down
to you. Be master over your brethren and let your
mother's sons bow down to you. Cursed be everyone
who curses you, and blessed be those who bless you"*
(Genesis 27:18-27).

Isaac had discernment in this story but he chose to overlook it.
He had a few checkmarks going on in his spirit but he chose to
believe the lies. The enemy is a good liar. He fools many of us
through his deception. Remember that Isaac's eyes had gone dim.
When our eyes are dim to spiritual discernment the enemy has us

just where he wants us and he will surely pull the wool over our eyes!

Isaac was alerted in his spirit. His first check mark was when he said, *"How is it you found it so quickly, my son?"* Isaac thought it strange that Esau could have hunted the game, then cleaned and prepared it so quickly. It seemed a little suspicious. Yet a lie was quickly given to divert his attention. Jacob said, "Because the Lord your God brought it to me." The enemy will even go as far as bringing God into the situation to keep you from seeing through to the truth.

Isaac's second check mark was when he said, *"The voice is Jacob's voice, but the hands are the hands of Esau."* Isaac still had his concerns. There was still something not right, conflicting in his spirit. The words sounded good, yet it didn't sound like his son Esau; however, the hands felt like his hands.

There are many times that we will be presented with conflicting circumstances. This could be God alerting us and we must hear by the Spirit and not with our natural minds.

The third check mark is when he asks, *"Are you really my son Esau?"* Isaac still feels a little unsettled about this situation. He is definitely discerning something, but all the outward signs are pointing to Jacob being Esau. Isaac finally disregards the discernment and is deceived by Jacob. He gives Jacob the blessing that was intended for Esau.

There is another story from scripture that reveals the importance of paying attention to our discernment. This can be found in Joshua chapter nine. This is the story of when all the kings of the surrounding nations wanted to gather together to fight against Israel. The inhabitants of Gibeon knew what God had done for Joshua and the Israelites and they feared they might be defeated by them just like those at Jericho and Ai. So they worked craftily (isn't that just like our enemy?) and pretended to be ambassadors. Once again, deception was their intention. They took worn-out clothes and moldy bread with them so it would look like they traveled from a far country. The rest is as follows:

And they went to Joshua, to the camp at Gilgal, and said to him and to the men of Israel, "We have come from a far country; now therefore, make a covenant with us." Then the men of Israel said to the Hivites, "Perhaps you dwell among us; so how can we make a covenant with you?" But they said to Joshua, "We are your servants." And Joshua said to them, "Who are you, and where do you come from?" So they said to him: "From a very far country your servants have come, because of the name of the Lord your God; for we have heard of His fame, and all that He did in Egypt, and all that He did to the two kings of the Amorites who were beyond the Jordan – to Sihon king of Heshbon, and Og king of Bashan, who was at Astaroth. Therefore our elders and all the inhabitants of our country spoke to us, saying, 'take provision with you for the journey, and go to meet them, and say to them, "We are your servants; now therefore, make a covenant with us."' "This bread of ours we took hot for our provision from our houses on the day we departed to come to you. But now look, it is dry and moldy. And these wineskins which we filled were new, and see, they are torn; and these our garments and our sandals have become old because of the very long journey." Then the men of Israel took some of their provisions; but they did not ask counsel of the Lord. So Joshua made peace with them, and made a covenant with them to let them live; and the rulers of the congregation swore to them (Joshua 9:6-15).

Once again, we see the enemy bringing deception. God was warning the Israelites through discernment, but again they chose to overlook the discernment and they entered into an unholy alliance. We see from this scripture that the first check mark came when the men of Israel said to the Hivites, *"Perhaps you dwell among us; so how can we make a covenant with you?"* Of course, they also brought the Lord into the conversation to divert their attention. Works like a charm! Just start talking our language and the enemy has us thinking – how could I think such bad thoughts about this person – they appear to be godly just like me.

In response to Joshua's question, the Gibeonites lie. They draw his attention to what is seen in the natural circumstances: moldy bread, old wineskins, and worn-out garments. This is a snare of the enemy. He wants to convince us that our concerns have us over-reacting. He does this by having us focus on what we see with our natural eye. Discernment doesn't come through the natural mind; it is placed there by the Spirit. For this reason we are to walk by the Spirit, not by the natural man.

> *But the natural man does not receive the things of the Spirit of God for they are foolishness to him; nor can he know them, because they are spiritually discerned* (I Corinthians 2:14).

The Gibeonites wanted to divert the discernment and make them look foolish for not recognizing all the signs that pointed to them coming from a far-off country. Whenever we disregard our discernment, we are now walking by the natural man and it seems foolish to us for thinking anything other than what is being said or done. Thus, Joshua and the Israelites made an unhealthy alliance with these people.

Joshua made a covenant with a foreign people without God's approval. *"But they did not ask the council of the Lord."* Whenever we are getting a check in our spirit and all the circumstances are telling us that everything is ok, we must inquire council from the Lord. When I am discerning something and no one else around me seems to be seeing what I am seeing, I always go before the Lord asking if this is Him bringing the alarm. God seems always ready to confirm to me when I ask Him. When I have chosen to go with what I see in the natural and disregard the discernment given, it never fails that I run into some trouble that could have been avoided.

Part of maturing in discernment is to come into a balance. The pendulum must swing and land in the middle. We need to swing from always seeing a demon behind every bush to properly discerning. And for those who are less discerning, we need to pay attention to those check marks in our spirit and ask God for counsel before we dismiss our discernment.

Chapter Five

Watchman Responsibilities

In chapter two, I wrote about the scriptures out of Ezekiel chapters three and thirty-three in which God called Ezekiel and made him a watchman for the house of Israel. His responsibility was to hear a word from God's mouth and warn the people for Him. If he did not warn the people and they died in their sin, Ezekiel was held responsible for the blood of these people. Likewise, if he did warn them and they did not turn from their evil ways, then Ezekiel was no longer responsible for their blood. However, this was not the only responsibility that Ezekiel had as a watchman. There are more responsibilities that the watchman has than just to report a word to the leaders.

Prayer

In the last chapter, I shared that one of the most important characteristics of watchmen is that they should be a person of prayer. Watchmen have the responsibility to pray. I have already discussed how necessary it is for watchmen to *"listen carefully with great care"* to see what the Lord might be saying concerning something they have discerned. This is our starting point of prayer. Many times we lack understanding and we need to pray that we might receive the understanding of the revelation we have been given. Prayer is the key to unlock the mysteries set before us. When we do not have the understanding of what we are seeing, prayer will help us become more enlightened. Prayer is the only way that we are going to receive the wisdom to know whether or not the revelation given is to be reported or not.

The first thing that we need to do when we receive a word from the Lord is to pray and ask God for the understanding of what He has just given us. Often times, this will mean waiting on the Lord for our answers. We need to pray even if we do not feel the burden to pray. It is our responsibility to pray. When we do not know what to pray, we can pray in the Holy Spirit. Romans 8:26-27 states:

> *"Likewise the Spirit also helps in our weaknesses. For we do not know what we should pray for as we ought, but the Spirit Himself makes intercession for us with groanings which cannot be uttered. Now He who searches the hearts knows what the mind of the Spirit is, because He makes intercession for the saints according to the will of God."*

We do not necessarily have to know how to pray because the Spirit knows and He will do the interceding. We just need to be the vessel that will allow Him to pray through us. God is searching to and fro throughout this earth looking for someone who will stand in the gap for Him. We can stand in the gap whether we know what to pray or not by yielding ourselves to Him and praying in the Spirit.

When we lack understanding and are praying in the Spirit, we can meditate on the revelation He has given and ask ourselves some important questions. If your revelation came in the way of a dream or a vision, then you need to know if the information is symbolic or literal? Most dreams and visions should not be taken literally. Ninety percent of my dreams are symbolic while only ten percent are literal or directly mean what was shown in the dream.

> *"I have also spoken by the prophets, and have multiplied visions; **I have given symbols** through the witness of the prophets"* (Hosea 12:10).

It is important for us to learn to think symbolically. We need to develop a symbolic mental attitude or we may miss what God is saying. I first search for a symbolic meaning to my dreams and then if I do not find one, I begin to think God may have spoken a literal word to me. I teach more on this subject and share tools to interpreting dreams in my book, *Parables in the Night Seasons: Understanding Your Dreams.*

Another question you may want to ask God is whether the revelation given is for now or in the future? Because the revelation can come with an urgency in the Spirit, we can think that it is a "now" word when it is actually for the future. We must not forget that because of the high place on the wall, the watchman can see something long before it reaches the city. In Dutch Sheets book, Watchman Prayer, he says:

> *"Sometimes watchmen receive words from the Holy Spirit and have difficulty discerning the timing. I have received warnings from them about situations they thought to be current, which in reality were concerning the future. Had we not discerned this, we would have discarded the warnings altogether because they made no sense at the time they were issued."* [1]

God may be alerting you to something the enemy intends to try to do later and it is not actually something that is happening right now. For example, you may have had a few dreams concerning an elder in your church that indicate this elder is having an affair; however, this does not necessarily mean that the elder is actually having an affair. Perhaps the Lord is showing you that the enemy is going to try to cause this person to fall in the area of sexual temptation. Just because we may have seen this outcome in a dream does not mean that it has happened. We need to pray for discernment as to whether this is a planned attack of the enemy against the person or whether the person is truly having an affair. Our prayers can stop the enemy from gaining victory over the believer. We must be careful not to make more out of the revelation than has been given us. Someone's reputation may be at stake here. If we want to grow in the things of the Lord, then we will need to be responsible with what He has given us.

You may also want to ask yourself if this revelation appears to affect the body corporately? Or does this information affect only the one for whom the revelation has been discerned? This will help you in determining whether or not your revelation needs to be reported. If the understanding you receive deals with the corporate body then you may have need to report it; however, if it deals only with the person whom the revelation was discerned then prayer may be all you need to do.

Whenever we are dealing with any negative revelation concerning a person, we must be sure to separate the individual from the spirits that may be operating in or through him or her. We have the ability to take authority and bind any spirit that may be operating in a person or situation. We can also pray that the individual involved would receive a revelation of their error and thereby receive healing and deliverance.

If the revelation comes in a dream, we must also ask whether the people represented portray themselves or represent someone else. This is very important to understanding our revelation. Oftentimes the people represented in a dream are symbolic of someone else or another situation. We cannot take the people represented at face value but must seek the Lord as to whom or what the dream is revealing.

When trying to determine whether or not to report a revelation, you may want to ask whether this appears to be urgent? (Remember we must beware of reporting brush fires. We want to be sure that we only report those that pose a real fire.) Also ask yourself, "Is my own heart right?" "Would I have the right motivation for sharing this information with the leaders?" If our hearts are not pure then we will most likely miss the understanding of our revelation or report it in a prideful way. We must have the redemptive heart of God in every situation we are called to report to the leaders.

Proper timing is so important when having to report a revelation. The right timing can have a lot to do with how your revelation is received by your leader. Ask God to reveal to you the proper time to sound the alarm.

When you have a witness to share your revelation with your leader you must approach him or her with a humble heart. Give the information you have and any understanding you have received. Do not add what you do not know. If the leader has questions for you, answer them. Once you have reported, unless asked by the leader, your job is completed. You have delivered the mail and they are now responsible for opening it up and doing something with it.

Always pray for your leader, regardless of his or her reaction to your revelation. Your leader has a great responsibility before God and needs your prayers. Always keep a humble heart before God and your leaders. Remember that we only know in part and we need to be responsible with the part God has given us as individuals.

Prayer can accomplish much. Prayer is the pre-requisite to power. Prayer gives us the power to see different situations overturned. Let us move on to maturity and become a people of prayer.

Know Your Sphere of Authority

The role of a watchman can differ in each individual. Some may have been called to be a personal watchman. This would mean that God alerts them to things concerning a specific person. For some, God has made them a watchman over a ministry or church. Others may have been given the role of watchman over a city or region. Whatever the case, we must be sure that we understand what sphere we are in and be careful not to go out of our sphere of authority.

When I was first alerted as a watchman, the role was over my family. After I understood this sphere of authority, God expanded my sphere to include friends and acquaintances. In time, the sphere increased such that God placed an anointing of the watchman on me to include specific ministries and churches. Since then, He has increased the anointing and I have more regional influence as well as to the body of Christ as a whole. This did not happen all at once. As I became more obedient and responsible with what God had given me, He expanded my sphere of authority. "Those who are faithful in the little shall receive much."

Again I have found Rick Joyner's article on "The Perfect Storms" published *in The Morning Star Prophetic Bulletin* to be of value here. Under the subtitle "Discerning Our Authority" he writes:

> *"The Lord is raising up different people to have authority over different areas. Some may have a special burden for diseases and plagues, while others may specialize in watching over political trends. Some are called to be watchmen over schools, who watch and pray for the schools in their neighborhood, or maybe even in their city. As they grow they may be given increasing spiritual authority over education in their nation. Others who are called as watchmen over their offices will grow to have authority over companies and will grow up even further to become seers for the whole industries."* [2]

We need to realize that if we move out of our sphere of authority, we are asking for trouble. We may still discern things that are out of our sphere, but there will not be the anointing upon us if we try to exercise authority out of the realm God has given us. I have heard of stories of so-called watchmen or prophets going to leaders of churches in their areas and even outside their areas with heavy words of doom and gloom to those ministries. These people have gone as far as saying that if the word of the Lord through them was not heeded, the wrath of God would come upon the minister and their ministry. From my experience, God rarely sends a watchman to a ministry with a heavy word where a relationship has not already been established. And if He should, then the person He has sent has already been recognized in the body of Christ as a spokesperson for the Lord and they are much more humble in the delivery of the word.

When we step out of our sphere of authority, we become fair game for the enemy. There is enough warfare when operating in your sphere that we do not need to open ourselves up for more by trying to exert our authority where it has not been given. Much of the warfare that we do experience when we are operating in our sphere is allowed by God to help train our hands to war in the Spirit. The warfare that will come against us when we step out of our sphere of authority will be without protection and ultimately leave us as a wounded soldier.

Understanding the Role of Your Leader

Before the Lord actually put me into the role of a leader, I would look at other leaders and believe that I could do a better job. Not only was this pride, but it was also ignorance. I had no clue what responsibility lay upon a leader. It was a different story when God appointed me to lead His people. I quickly learned that the role entailed much more than I had known. I found myself repenting often for judging any other leader. We must understand the role of a leader so that we can operate effectively as a watchman.

The leader has been commissioned by God to lead the people. He has also been given the responsibility for the spiritual well-being of the sheep.

> *"Obey those who rule over you, and be submissive, for they watch out for your souls, as those who must give account. Let them do so with joy and not with grief, for that would be unprofitable for you"* (Hebrews 13:17).

God has given your leader the responsibility to watch out for your soul, not only your soul, but also the souls of all that have been given to his or her flock. They are accountable before God for these souls. This is a very serious matter before God. We are exhorted then to let them do their job with joy and not to give them grief because then it becomes unprofitable for us.

> *"My brethren, let not many of you become teachers, knowing that we shall receive a stricter judgment"* (James 3:1).

What a responsibility before God! Your leader will receive a stricter judgment. When God placed me as a leader, I took this passage very seriously. That is probably why I repented so often for judging other leaders. The job is not an easy task. Let us not think more highly than we ought as though we could do things better. Again, we need to cover our leaders in prayer. This is the best thing we can do for them. Let us become a blessing to our leaders.

Understanding the Spiritual Authority of the Leader

When God commissioned your leader for his or her role, He also placed an anointing upon them. No one else has been given the anointing for his or her specific task. God also gives the leader vision for their ministry. All authority has been given to your leader for the ministry that has been placed on him.

We must be careful as watchmen that we do not try to assume the role of our leader. When we have been given revelation to report, we have the anointing to carry this information whether our leaders receive it or not. Your anointing as a watchman lies in the reporting; their anointing lies in the decisions concerning the revelation you bring. If the leader chooses to do nothing concerning the revelation you have given them, it is their responsibility before God.

---

[1] Dutch Sheets, *Watchman Prayer* (Ventura, CA: Regal Books, 2000), p. 176.
[2] Rick Joyner, The Perfect Storms, *The Morning Star Prophetic Bulletin,* March 2003. Used by permission. www.morningstarministries.org

Chapter Six

Watchman, Walk in Your Authority

Many people have walked in fear of our adversary. It is true that our enemy is real. His job is to kill, steal and destroy but as watchman we should not be in fear of him. At the same time, we cannot be ignorant to his schemes. We need to develop a healthy perspective of who our enemy is and what he is capable of, but we also need to have a divine perspective of who we are in Christ. When we come into an understanding of who we are in Christ, we will not walk in fear of our enemy.

Do Not Be Afraid

Satan once dwelled in the presence of the Lord, but because he wanted to be exalted as God, he was cast down to earth. He became a "god" of this world. This world is where he dwells and where his realm of authority is. His job is to kill, steal and destroy. However, Jesus came to earth, died on the cross, took victory over Satan and was given all authority over heaven and earth and all the principalities and powers of the air, which includes Satan and his demons. We as believers have also been given authority over our enemy. The following scriptures are in Jesus' words:

> *"Behold I give you the authority to trample on serpents and scorpions, and over all the power of the enemy, and nothing shall by any means hurt you"* (Luke 10:19).

"And these signs will follow those who believe: In My name they will cast out demons; they will speak with new tongues; they will take up serpents; and if they drink anything deadly, it will by no means hurt them; they will lay hands on the sick and they will recover" (Mark 16:17,18).

God has given us authority over the enemy. It is as though God has given us a "power of attorney" in order for us to exercise authority in His name whenever we should have need. Webster's dictionary defines "power of attorney" as a written legal authorization for another person to act in one's place. Jesus has given us the legal authorization to act in His place. The problem is that most of us do not act upon or exercise our authority. Most likely it is because we have not really understood how much authority we carry. We need to get this understanding imparted into us. God has given us the authority in His name to act as He would act towards the enemy. It has nothing to do with us, but everything to do with Him.

Authority through the Blood

One day I was driving down a two-lane road when a police officer passed me from the opposite direction. Immediately I reduced my speed. I don't know if I was speeding, but it has become my instant reaction whenever I see a policeman while driving. The reason, of course, is that I recognize that they have the authority to pull me over and write me a speeding ticket if I am indeed speeding. The key here is that I recognized the authority the policeman carried as an officer of the law. We need to learn from this example. Our enemy recognizes the authority we carry as believers. He trembles because of it. However, if we do not understand our authority and walk in it, he will try to outwit us and cause fear to grip us, leaving us paralyzed and defeated. We need to remember that "greater is He that is in us than he that is in this world" and that all authority has been given us through the blood of Jesus.

Let's take the example of the police officer a step further. When an officer of the law is sworn in to do his duty as a representative of our government, he doesn't necessarily recognize right away all the authority he carries. He may know that as an officer he will receive authority, but experientially he will not yet understand it. He may have gone through the necessary training, but not until he puts on his uniform and goes into the field representing the law enforcement will he actually recognize how people respond to his uniform. The people recognize his authority by the clothes he is wearing (in my case, by the car he was driving!). He then sees the response of others' to his given authority and it builds his confidence. He becomes aware through others responses to him that he truly carries the authority that has been placed on him. So much so, that when he is not wearing his uniform or driving the government vehicle, he still understands he carries this authority and walks in it.

Likewise, we have been sworn into the government of the Kingdom of God. We are representatives of Jesus our King. He has given us authority over the kingdom of this world through the blood of Jesus and the power of His name. We are being trained through the Word of God to walk as His representatives. The blood of Jesus is the garment of authority that we wear. We have the right to exercise our authority based on what He did for us. We can use the power of attorney and act in His name. Satan and his demons see this garment of the blood of Jesus and they must fall under His authority. They know that His name is exalted above any other name and that every knee must bow, even the knee of our enemy!

Satan trembles at the blood of Jesus and at the hearing of His Name. Sometimes I picture the enemy and his demons squealing at the sound of His name or when they come in contact with the power of the blood of Jesus. The picture I get is that of the wicked witch from the <u>Wizard of Oz</u>. When the scarecrow, the tin man and the lion rescued Dorothy from the bondage of the evil witch, they accidentally threw water on the witch. She then began to scream and squeal loudly that she was melting, melting, melting, until the only thing left was her wicked-looking hat on the ground. This is the picture I envision of the enemy when we exercise our authority through the blood of Jesus and by His name. I just picture the devil squealing, "I'm melting, melting, melting, my power and strength is melting." Satan's power cannot stand against the power of the blood and the name of Jesus. We leave Satan trembling until he can no longer use his power over us. We need to practice walking with our garments of authority and watch for the defeated response of our enemy.

When God wanted me to understand the authority of His name, He put me on a journey to see His power at hand. I used to be a person of great fear. Fear would grip and even paralyze me. God did not give me this spirit of fear, but rather of power, love and a sound mind. However, it took me a while to realize I could experience the power, love and a sound mind, instead of a fear-gripping dread! God started to reveal to me the fear I had through dreams. These dreams appeared to be demonic in nature but I believe it was my training ground by which I was able to overcome fear and recognize the power in the name and blood of Jesus.

In one dream, I saw a spirit hovering over me and felt so paralyzed by it that I was hardly able to speak the name of Jesus. Only after much effort was I able to get the name "Jesus" to escape from my vocal cords. Upon waking, I felt defeated realizing that as a child of the living God I should not be in fear and should have no problem using the name of Jesus to help me. God brought this revelation to me and then continued to give me similar dreams. In each dream, I grew stronger and bolder in my spirit. It became easier to declare the name of Jesus, and every time I did the spirit would have to flee! Once I was so angry with the enemy that I spoke matter-of-factly ordering him to leave because of the authority that had been given me by Jesus! I no longer feared the enemy or what he might think he could do to me. God helped me to come to that realization through these seemingly demonic dreams. I am not saying it wasn't difficult to have those dreams, and there are times when the hair on the back of my neck can stand up, but I now know the authority I have been given through the name and blood of Jesus. It sends the enemy squealing, "I'm melting, melting, melting, my power and strength is melting!"

In Deut. 7:16-26, God gives us an illustration of the authority He has given the Israelites. We can also apply these scriptures to the watchman. It reads,

> "*Also you shall destroy all the peoples whom the Lord your God delivers over to you; your eye shall have no pity on them; nor shall you serve their gods, for that will be a snare to you. If you should say in your heart, 'These nations are greater than I; how can I dispossess them?' – you shall not be afraid of them, but you shall remember well what the Lord your God did to Pharaoh and to all Egypt; the great trials which your eyes saw, the signs and the wonders, the mighty hand and the outstretched arm, by which the Lord your God brought you out. So shall the Lord your God do to all the peoples of whom you are afraid. Moreover the Lord your God will send the hornet among them until those who are left, who hide themselves from you, are destroyed. You shall not be terrified of them; for the Lord your God, the great and awesome God, is among you. And the Lord your God will drive out those nations before you little by little; you will be unable to destroy them at once, lest the beasts of the field become too numerous for you. But the Lord your God will deliver them over to you, and will inflict defeat upon them until they are destroyed. And He will deliver their kings into your hand, and you will destroy their name from under heaven; no one shall be able to stand against you until you have destroyed them. You shall burn the carved images of their gods with fire; you shall not covet the silver or gold that is on them, nor take it for yourselves, lest you be snared by it; for it is an abomination to the Lord your God. Nor shall you bring an abomination into your house, lest you be doomed to destruction like it. You shall utterly detest it and utterly abhor it, for it is an accursed thing.*"

Although these scriptures were written to the children of Israel as an exhortation for them to not fear the peoples of the land they were about to enter, we as watchman can also be exhorted by them. God was letting the children of Israel know that whatever obstacle they came against, that they were to drive it out of their land and their lives because God was among them. I think we can take this same exhortation and use it towards the enemy and anything he should use in trying to devour our lives. As watchmen, we receive much revelation as to what the enemy is plotting against the body of Christ, or the specific ministry we are involved in. We need to remember that God is among and in us, and by His authority we are able to drive out the inhabitants or spirits that are trying to hinder the work of the ministry.

Basically the Lord is saying that He will deliver the spirits over to us, and we shall destroy all of them. God will bring forth the revelation of the hindering spirits and we then shall be the ones who destroy them. We are not to pity the spirits or they will become a snare to us. God is going to reveal the spirits operating and it is our responsibility to destroy them. How do we destroy them? We pray through the power of the blood of Jesus and in His name. Again, God exhorts us not to pity the spirit otherwise they could become a snare to us. One of Webster's definitions for snare is "anything serving to entrap, entangle, or catch unawares." If we do not go after the things God has delivered to us, we will end up being entrapped by them.

God also encourages us in these scriptures not to be afraid, but to remember well what the Lord our God has done for us in times past. We need to remember the testimonies of God's greatness as we have read from the Word and have experienced in our own lives. God will defeat the enemy that you may fear, just as He has done in times past. He made a public spectacle of Satan. The Lord will also give you discernment for those spirits who hide themselves from you. The Lord says in verse twenty-two that He will drive them out little by little. We don't have to worry about having too many to deal with at one time (thank you Lord!). God will not give us more than we can handle. This is our training ground! The Lord is the one who delivers the enemy into our hands. Verse twenty-three in the Amplified Version says, *"But the Lord your God will give them over to you and will confuse them with a mighty panic until they are destroyed."* This is what happens in the spirit when you know your authority. The enemy is confused with a mighty panic! I like that! Let's send the enemy running in confusion with a mighty panic.

God is also saying that He will deliver over to you their kings, which I would call the strongman. He delivers them over to you through discernment, but you must destroy their name from under heaven. When God discloses a spirit that is operating or even the strongman, then it is our responsibility to destroy their works through the power of the blood of Jesus and through His name. If we allow the spirits to stay, we may be doomed to destruction like them. We must utterly detest and abhor the spirits and be careful to love the people through whom they are operating. God delivers them to us and we must use our authority through prayer to utterly destroy the enemy.

Chapter Seven

Strengthening Our Foundation

About a year and a half ago, I felt the Lord gave me an object lesson through some unfortunate circumstances in my life. At that time, my doctor reported to me that the results of my bone scan indicated severe osteoporosis. He warned me that my bones had weakened and that they could snap and break very easily, even by bumping something. He added that forty percent of those with osteoporosis die as a result of the break. (This was definitely not what I wanted to hear!) He said all this to emphasize the need for a plan of action to stop the bone weakening and perhaps even strengthen them and build new bone. This would require my taking high doses of calcium and a prescription that is designed to help build bone.

I was discouraged by what I heard because I felt I was much too young for such a medical condition. His words of warnings about what I could and couldn't do kept ringing in my ears reminding me that this would be a lifelong journey to keep my bones from breaking.

Normally I would have taken this report as something personal, but what happened next caused me to press in for some answers. Within a few hours of my report, I received a call from my son's school telling me that my fourteen-year-old son had slipped on some gravel and broke his arm. When some of my other children had bone breaks, it took an x-ray to confirm it. While I am talking with my son's PE teacher, I asked him if he was sure that my son's arm was broken. He emphatically said, "Yes" and I rushed to the school to pick up my son. To my horror, I saw there that I wouldn't be picking up my son, nor anyone else except an ambulance! There lay my son on the ground in severe pain with his hand detached from his arm, no bone holding the two parts together. It actually looked like rubber between his hand and arm since the bone had completely snapped in two. En route to the hospital, the ambulance attendants tried to reassure my son and I that he would be just fine. From what I had seen, I found little comfort in their words. My son was in excruciating pain and I had no way to offer him tangible hope and comfort. I am glad to report that after two surgeries and months of healing, my son has full function of his hand and arm. I praise God for bringing healing to his bones!

Strong Foundation

So what was the object lesson of this story and what does it have to do with the importance of the watchman role? After things settled concerning my son's injury, I began to ask God some nagging questions. Why did my son with perfectly healthy bones break his arm, when the doctor had said it was my bones that were weak and could break so easily? Why did this happen on the very day of the doctor's report? It did not seem like a coincidence. I felt there had to be more than personal meaning to this. So I pressed into God and asked Him to relate it to me.

Do you know that sometimes God will have certain people "walk out" in the natural what is happening in the spiritual? He did so with the prophets of old, such as Hosea. God had Hosea marry a prostitute because the spiritual condition of the children of Israel was that of harlotry (Hosea 1:3). This is what you would term a "prophetic enactment." Likewise, God called Ezekiel to prophetic enactments and made him a sign to the house of Israel (Ezekiel 12:6). (Stay with me as I share how this applies!)

As you think about our bodies, you will note that the bones are the structure or very foundation. Lacking bones, we would have a hard time being held together. Spiritually speaking, the bones are the foundation of the body of Christ. When the foundation (bones) are weakened, they present a danger of being broken which could in some cases lead to death (remember my doctor's report concerning the osteoporosis). The body of Christ has need of strong healthy bones in order to prevent a break or death in a church or ministry.

Someone with Osteoporosis is not aware of the condition without a bone density report. Osteoporosis is called the "silent disease." Many people are not even given a bone scan until they are elderly. By then, a break is usually what alerts the doctors to do a scan. My scan came because I requested it after hearing about bone loss regarding a healthy friend. I knew that I lacked enough calcium in my diet because of a seven-year lactose intolerance, (I've since been healed of this intolerance and am now praising God every time I eat dairy products!) so I requested a bone density test.

I believe that the body of Christ is not as healthy as it may think. To a degree, it is suffering from a silent spiritual disease. I believe that the foundation of the church is in a very weakened state. If we are not careful, the foundation will break which could lead to spiritual "death." The reason for this condition is the enemy has found ways to sneak into our churches and weaken it's foundation.

How was the enemy able to do this? It is because the watchmen have not been on the wall reporting the impending danger the enemy has planned against the church. Some watchmen are reporting, yet many leaders are not hearing or responding to the reports. Because the various ministries are not functioning properly, the enemy has been able to weaken the structure and we have had a silent disease penetrate the very foundation of the church. We can do something about this, but it is urgent we start now.

When I was given my osteoporosis report, I was also given a bone-building prescription and advised to take a daily high dose of calcium. If I wanted to see my bones strengthen and rebuild, it was imperative that I started immediately with my doctor's advice.

Likewise, God is our heavenly doctor who has given us the prescription to help build those weakened bones or the weakened foundation of the church. I believe the prescription has to do with the working relationship between the watchman and the leaders of the church, making this book a timely prescription to the body of

Christ. If we can learn the roles of both watchmen and leaders and implement them in the body of Christ, we will not only keep our bones from becoming weakened, but will actually strengthen and build them. The results will be a healthy new foundation.

One of the things that my son's orthopedic surgeon said during the recovery of my son's arm was that the new bone would be stronger than before. This too is a "word" to the body of Christ. If we will begin to take the prescribed remedy the Lord is offering us for the health of the body of Christ, we too will see the new bone (or foundation) become stronger than before.

On a positive note, I had a dream recently in which I had a new bone density report that showed I gained ten percent of the bone back. I believe this is not only literal of what I can expect from my next density report, but it is also showing that God intends to build up the foundations of our churches as we are faithful to take the prescription He has given. Let's start today with implementing the truths of this book.

Chapter Eight

Rebuilding the Wall

In order for us to build a stronger healthier body, we will need to be aware of those forces that come against the work of the Lord. We need to know where the foxes have found their way into our ministries and churches. The only way that we will begin to see where the weakened structures are is to set our watchmen on the walls where they belong. However, this can only be done if we have walls to set them on. It is time for us to rebuild the walls around our churches and ministries. They have been broken down and have need of rebuilding.

Keep the Foxes Out

There was a time when the children of Israel were instructed to rebuild the broken down walls of the city of Jerusalem. This came through the burden that Nehemiah carried. The book of Nehemiah is all about the rebuilding of the walls of Jerusalem. In Nehemiah 1:1-3 we read:

> *The words of Nehemiah the son of Hachaliah. It came to pass in the month of Chislev, in the twentieth year, as I was in Shushan the citadel, that Hanani one of my brethren came with men from Judah; and I asked them concerning the Jews who had escaped, who had survived the captivity, and concerning Jerusalem. And they said to me, "The survivors who*

are left from the captivity in the province are there in
great distress and reproach. *The wall of Jerusalem
is also broken down, and its gates are burned with
fire."*

The walls of Jerusalem were broken down which caused great
distress and reproach upon the survivors who had been taken captive
by the king of Babylon. Nehemiah had great concern for the welfare
of Jerusalem and the children of Israel. Upon hearing the words of
Hanani, the burden of the Lord for Jerusalem and the children of
Israel came upon him. You can feel his concern and burden through
his prayer in Nehemiah 1:4-11:

*So it was, when I heard these words, that **I sat down
and wept and mourned for many days; I was fasting
and praying before the God of heaven**. And I said:
"I pray, Lord God of heaven, O great and awesome
God, You who keep Your covenant and mercy with
those who love You and observe Your commandments,
please let Your ear be attentive and Your eyes open,
that You may hear the prayer of Your servant which I
pray before You now, day and night, for the children
of Israel Your servants, and confess the sins of the
children of Israel which we have sinned against You.
Both my father's house and I have sinned. We have
acted very corruptly against You, and have not kept
the commandments, the statutes, nor the ordinances
which You commanded Your servant Moses.
Remember, I pray the word that you commanded
Your servant Moses, saying, 'If you are unfaithful, I
will scatter you among the nations; but if you return
to Me, and keep My commandments and do them,
though some of you were cast out to the farthest part
of the heavens, yet I will gather them from there, and
bring them to the place which I have chosen for My
name.' Now these are Your servants and Your people,*

whom You have redeemed by Your great power, and
by Your strong hand. O Lord, I pray, please let our
ear be attentive to the prayer of Your servant, and to
the prayer of Your servants who desire to fear Your
name; and let Your servant prosper this day, I pray
and grant him mercy in the sight of this man." For I
was the king's cupbearer.

Nehemiah's burden was so great that he felt the urgent need to
return to his homeland. He went before King Artaxerxes, who was
reigning at the time and made his request to return to Jerusalem.
God gave him favor with the king and his request was granted.
Nehemiah's intentions upon returning to Jerusalem were to gather
his countrymen and commission them to rise up and rebuild the
shattered walls that lay in ruins.

Then I said to them, "You see the distress that we
are in, how Jerusalem lies waste, and its gates are
*burned with fire. **Come and let us build the wall of***
Jerusalem that we may no longer be a reproach."
And I told them of the hand of my God which had
been good upon me, and also of the king's words that
*he had spoken to me. **So they said, "Let us rise up***
and build." Then they set their hands to this good
work (Nehemiah 2:17,18).

When our walls lay in ruins, it brings a reproach upon our
churches and ministries. We need to feel the burden as Nehemiah
did. We need to rise up and rebuild the walls so that our watchmen
may return to their positions and we can turn the reproach from us.

The rebuilding of the wall is a good work and we must set our
minds and hands to the rebuilding of it. This work will require
everyone's involvement. We need the watchmen, the intercessors
and the leaders to work together in the rebuilding process. Much
can be accomplished through a spirit of unity.

We can expect that the rebuilding will bring opposition from our enemy. He will use many scare tactics to discourage us and to halt the rebuilding process of the wall. However, I believe we can learn much from Nehemiah's journey and apply some of the principles from Nehemiah chapter 4 to help us in our endeavor to rebuild the walls of our churches and ministries.

> *But it so happened, when Sanballat heard that we were rebuilding the wall, that he was furious and very indignant and mocked the Jews. And he spoke before his brethren and the army of Samaria, and said, "What are these feeble Jews doing?* ***Will they fortify themselves?*** *Will they offer sacrifices? Will they complete it in a day? Will they revive the stones from the heaps of rubbish – stones that are burned?" Now Tobiah the Ammonite was beside him, and he said, "Whatever they build, if even a fox goes up on it, he will break down their stone wall"* (Nehemiah 4:1-3).

Sanballat, his brethren and the army of Samaria came against the work of rebuilding the wall. Nehemiah encountered an attack from his enemies and so will we. Sanballat, his brethren and the army of Samaria are a type of Satan, his demons and evil hordes. Attacks will always come our way when we begin to move into what God is calling us to do. In the rebuilding of the wall, we will be fortifying our churches and ministries and this makes the enemy very angry!

When the enemy hears that we are rebuilding our walls, he will become furious and indignant and even mock us. The enemy will even try to make us doubt our ability to do this work. Just as Sanballat said, "What are these feeble Jews doing?", our enemy will mock us the same way. However, I Corinthians 1:27,28 states:

> *"But God has chosen the foolish things of this world to put to shame the wise, and God has chosen the weak things of the world to put to shame the things which are mighty; and the base things of the world*

and the things which are despised God has chosen,
and the things which are not, to bring to nothing the
things that are."

It does not matter what kind of insults the enemy throws our way, or what he says to make us feel incapable of doing the work because God has said that He has chosen us foolish, weak feeble vessels to show His power through. When we come under attack from the assault of the enemy, we must do as Nehemiah did when his enemy brought forth his attack.

"Hear, O our God, for we are despised; turn their
reproach on their own heads and give them as plunder
to a land of captivity! Do not cover their iniquity,
and do not let their sin be blotted out from before
*You; **for they have provoked You to anger before the***
***builders**" (Nehemiah 4:4,5).*

Nehemiah turned the enemy's threats into prayer. We must do the same. We need to remember that the enemy is not only provoking us, but also he is provoking God! We need to ask God to defend us in these situations and to release His warring angels to war on our behalf. We can defuse, diminish and halt an attack from the enemy through our prayers.

After Nehemiah prayed, he returned to the work of rebuilding the wall.

"So we built the wall, and the entire wall was joined
*together up to half its height, **for the people had a***
***mind to work**" (Nehemiah 4:6).*

What do we need to do in the midst of an attack from the enemy? We need to pray and continue to work. We must set our minds on the rebuilding of the walls. We must keep our minds fixed on God and continue to do what He is requiring of us. This does not mean though, that the enemy will not try another tactic to try to keep us from accomplishing the work. Note what happened next in Nehemiah's journey of the rebuilding of the wall:

> *"Now it happened, when Sanballat, Tobiah, the Arabs, the Ammonites, and the Ashdodites heard that* ***the walls of Jerusalem were being restored and the gaps were beginning to be closed,*** *that they became very angry, and all of them conspired together to come and attack Jerusalem and create confusion"* (Nehemiah 4:7-8).

Because the walls were being restored and the gaps were beginning to be closed, the enemy gathered what he could to come and attack the people and create confusion. It is possible during our time of rebuilding that the enemy will use this same strategy and try to create confusion among us. We must recognize the strategies of the enemy and once again do what Nehemiah did in chapter 4 verse 9:

> *"Nevertheless we made our prayer to our God and because of them we set a watch against them day and night."*

Nehemiah prays again in the midst of his attack and then he takes it a step further by setting a watch against the enemy both day and night. We must do the same. How do we set a watch against the enemy both day and night? We employ the watchmen to take their positions on the wall even if the wall is only up to half its height. The watchmen need to stay alert and pray. God will begin to reveal the plans and strategies of the enemy as we stay alert and continue in prayer. Many of the plans of the enemy will be revealed to us through dreams. God will alert his watchmen in the night seasons through dreams, exposing much through this avenue. It is important that we carefully consider the watchmen dreams and pray for understanding.

We must also keep our focus on rebuilding the wall. Since this will be new to most churches and ministries, we can find ourselves overwhelmed by the opposition and the work that is ahead of us. This was not foreign to Nehemiah and those who were working on the wall with him.

> *"Then Judah said, The strength of the laborers is failing, and there is so much rubbish that we are not able to build the wall"* (Nehemiah 4:10).

It is true that the strength of the laborers in God's kingdom can fail at times. This is when we must renew our strength in the joy of the Lord. We can do this by taking time to soak in God's presence. Not only should we set a watch both day and night, but also we must have our personal and corporate fellowship time with the Lord to be refreshed and to renew our strength. It is during these times of refreshing that we also receive the revelation concerning the enemy's plan of attack against us.

> *"And our adversaries said, they will neither know nor see anything, till we come into their midst and kill them and cause the work to cease. So it was when the Jews who dwelt near them came, that they told us ten times, from whatever place you turn they will be upon us"* (Nehemiah 4:11-12).

Here we see Nehemiah's adversaries plotting and thinking that the people will not know or see anything until they come into their midst to kill them and cause the work to cease. However, the Jews who dwelt near by came and warned them repeatedly about the enemy's plot. The same will happen for us. The enemy will think that he can outwit us, destroy the work and cause it to cease, but God will expose his plot to us through the watchmen. Generally it will come through more than one watchman; everything is established through two or three witnesses.

Nehemiah does not disregard the warnings from the Jews but takes their warnings to heart as he strengthens his position even more.

> *"Therefore I positioned men behind the lower parts*
> *of the wall, at the openings; and I set the people*
> *according to their families, with their swords, their*
> *spears, and their bow. And I looked, and arose and*
> *said to the nobles, to the leaders, and to the rest of*
> *the people, 'Do not be afraid of them. Remember*
> *the Lord, great and awesome, and fight for your*
> *brethren, your sons, your daughters, your wives and*
> *your houses'"* (Nehemiah 4:13,14).

Nehemiah gathers the people and sets them according to their families with their swords and spears. Basically, we can look at this spiritually and see the importance of gathering the watchmen, the intercessors and the leaders to pray and war against the enemy. Nehemiah encouraged the people by reminding them of how great and awesome their God is and how they must not be afraid of the enemy. We must also remember how great and awesome our God is. We cannot be afraid of the enemy's threats. We must fight for our churches and ministries. We must fight for our brethren. God will bring the enemy's plot to nothing if we will position ourselves and take our stand on the wall.

> *"And it happened, when our enemies heard that it*
> *was known to us, and* **that God had brought their**
> **plot to nothing,** *that all of us returned to the wall,*
> *everyone to his work"* (Nehemiah 4:15).

Can you see through these verses how the watchman and leadership roles are supposed to work? The watchmen report the warnings to the leader. The leader takes heed to the warning and he calls the troops in to prayer. The troops are the leaders, watchmen and the intercessors. The enemy then realizes that God has brought his plot to nothing! I love it. What the enemy had intended for harm, God exposed and brought his plan to no effect. We win! But we don't stop there. Now it is time for the watchmen to return to the wall and everyone else to the work God has called them to.

"So it was, from that time on, that half of my servants worked at construction, while the other half held the spears, the shields, the bows and wore armor; and the leaders were behind all the house of Judah. Those who built on the wall, and those who carried burdens, loaded themselves so that with one hand they worked at construction, and with the other held a weapon" (Nehemiah 4:16-18).

It is noteworthy that Nehemiah had half of his servants working at the construction of the wall, while the other half held the spears, the shields, the bows and wore armor. Also it says that the leaders were behind all the house of Judah.

Nehemiah knew the importance of having the people work in the area of their specific anointing. I believe the watchmen and leaders are to work at the construction of the wall while the intercessors remain armed with the spears, the shields, and the bows and wear the armor. This does not mean that the watchmen and leaders do not have responsibility in holding their weapons. As we can see from this those who worked at construction had one hand doing the work and their other hand holding a weapon.

We all must continue with the work of the Lord and we need to be sure that we are armed with the Sword of the Word at all times. We put one hand to the plow and the other hand is to be armed with the Sword of the Word for battle. For the Word of God is living and powerful, and sharper than any two-edged sword, piercing even to the division of soul and spirit, and joints and marrow, and is a discerner of the thoughts and intents of the heart. (Hebrews 4:12) The Sword of the Word is one of our weapons against the enemy.

I am impressed with the scripture that says the leaders were behind all the house of Judah. I take it that they believed in each person's anointing and they encouraged each of them in their specific tasks. Our leaders today must come behind their people, recognize the different anointings and encourage each of them in their specific duties, especially in this area of the watchmen and intercessors.

"Then I said to the nobles, the rulers, and the rest of the people, the work is great and extensive, and we are separated far from one another on the wall. Whenever you hear the sound of the trumpet, rally to us there. Our God will fight for us" (Nehemiah 4:19-20).

It is true that the work is great and extensive. It is when the sound of the trumpet is made that we are to rally together. I believe the trumpet is symbolic of the prophetic voice. When the watchmen begin to declare the warnings, it becomes like the sound of a trumpet, heralding the troops. When we rally together in prayer we must know that our God will fight for us no matter how difficult the situation may seem. Our job is to come together in prayer, intercede and watch our God fight on our behalf. God is training our hands for war.

As we come together, we must hear from the Lord the strategies of heaven concerning every situation and circumstance that has warranted a warning. God will give us His plan if we will inquire of Him. In the times that David was faced with battle, he inquired of the Lord to what He would say. David prevailed in battle whenever he inquired of the Lord. If he did not inquire of the Lord, he did not prevail in battle. When we rally together, we must inquire of the Lord for each specific battle. God is faithful to give us the wisdom and revelation needed for each battle plan.

"So we labored in the work, and half of the men held the spears from daybreak until the stars appeared. At the same time I also said to the people, let each man and his servant stay at night in Jerusalem, that they may be our guard by night and a working party by day. So neither I, my brethren, my servants, nor the men of the guard who followed me took off our clothes, except that everyone took them off for washing" (Nehemiah 4:21-23).

So we labor! Just as Nehemiah and the people with him labored, we must labor! We continue in the work of rebuilding the wall both day and night. It is important that we remain faithful.

Let us stand at our posts waiting to see what the Lord might show us just as in Habakkuk 2:1:

> *"I will stand my watch and set myself on the rampart, and watch to see what He will say to me, and what I will answer when I am corrected."*

With everyone doing their part, we can rebuild the walls of our churches and ministries. We can take away the reproach and make them a safe place for the brethren to dwell.

Chapter Nine

Leaders and Watchmen

In much of this book, I have been dealing specifically with the watchman and his role and relationship to the leader. In this chapter I want to direct my attention to the leader in relationship to the watchmen and what the leader should know.

What Leaders Need to Know

First of all, leaders, I want you to know that I am for you. I am also for the watchmen. Being a watchman myself helps me to understand their role and responsibilities. It is my desire to train the watchmen to be a blessing to their leaders in this gift they walk in. Yes, believe it or not, it is a gift! It is a gift to you, leaders.

For a long time I think that many leaders have thought the watchman to be their foe rather than their friend. But God has placed a special anointing and love in the watchman's heart for your ministry. Most watchmen do not understand why they feel such a great love for you or why they are so passionate about your ministry, but it is God endowed. God knew that you had a huge responsibility in being a leader and He knew you needed a helpmate so to speak. So He gave you watchmen.

For you, a watchman is like being given eyes behind your head. You are busy doing what God has called you to do and your job as a leader comes with great responsibilities. You are building His kingdom! Because your focus is about doing the Father's business, you will not always see what the enemy is plotting against you or your ministry behind your back. But your watchmen will.

The enemy does not like what you are doing and he is going to do everything possible to come against the work God has entrusted to you. God knew the enemy's plan to try and destroy you and your ministry so He enlisted some help for you. He gave you watchmen. The watchman anointing has been placed there to protect you and your ministry.

As I pointed out in chapter one, watchmen were employed both night and day to stand upon the highest part of the city wall to see if there were any enemies approaching the city or camp. Not only were these men able to see out beyond the city, they were also able to see what was going on inside the city. Because of the height of these walls, it made it easier for the watchmen to see afar off. Thus, upon the wall the watchmen were able to see potential danger approaching long before it reached the city. If they saw something suspicious, they needed to warn the king so the city could be prepared for an attack. This is the same for your watchmen. God has given your watchmen a special anointing to see far off in the distance, spiritually speaking, and they can often see approaching danger long before there is any evidence to you or others.

I believe this is the reason that many watchmen have been misunderstood. They have felt or seen an alert of potential danger coming from either within or without the camp. The revelations of warnings may have come in the form of a dream, vision or "knowing". Unfortunately often when watchmen have shared these warnings with their leaders, the leaders--not seeing what they are seeing--think that the watchmen are the ones bringing the problems into the camp. They get labeled as troublemakers. This could not be farther from the truth.

Leaders, it is important that you understand that the watchmen have been placed in your camp for your protection and the protection of your ministry. They are generally faithful and desire the very best for you. God has anointed them to see what you may not be able to see. God alerts the watchmen so that you might be prepared to fight against the attacks of the enemy. Every ministry has need of these watchmen.

Now it is true that an immature watchman can create problems. This is why it is so necessary for the leaders to train the watchmen in their roles. They need to be pastored and trained in their responsibility and gifting.

Once again, I want to recap on some of what Rick Joyner said in The Morning Star Prophetic Bulletin in March of 2003. Under the article entitled "The Perfect Storms" he writes concerning the watchman:

> *"Every congregation and city needs these spiritual watchmen in their places at this time.* ***Those who do not have them will be victims of what could have otherwise been prevented."***

> ***"All of these watchmen had to be trained in their duties***, *and commissioned by the leaders of the cities, the farmers whose fields they watched, or the leaders of the nation whose borders they patrolled.* ***Likewise, leaders of congregations, missions and all other ministries must invest in training and deploying watchmen or they are going to suffer increasing loss and unnecessary tragedies."*** [1]

Here Joyner stresses the importance of investing time and training for our watchmen. Watchmen are important to the overall functioning of your ministry. Without them, there is potential for destruction and as stated above, the possibility of suffering increasing loss and unnecessary tragedies. Such things can be prevented. Rick Joyner also states in the article:

> *"We must be able to see how things in the natural are reflected by spiritual realities. The church needs to then grow in faith and spiritual authority to affect the areas that we have been given to watch over.* ***This will usually come by the watchmen developing a good relationship with the elders*** *who are called to*

*'sit in the gates' or have authority to make judgments
over that domain."*

*"If we are becoming prophetic we should be able to
see farther and farther into the future so that we are
not continually surprised by events.   Then we can
also begin to pray earlier."*

Establishing Relationship with Your Watchmen

The relationship between the leaders and the watchmen in this
hour is very critical to the health of our churches and ministries. In
order for the health of the church to recover, the watchmen will need
to be able to function in their anointing. The watchmen must also be
allowed to report what they see as the Lord leads them.

Generally, God will raise up watchmen from within your ministry.
It is usually someone who has been a faithful member. It might seem
out of the ordinary for them to all of a sudden begin to bring alarming
revelation to you. You may even question what has triggered such
behavior. Rest assured in these cases, that God has probably made
them a watchman for you.

Most of the time, your watchmen will be those whom you have
established some sort of relationship with. Occasionally God may
bring you a seasoned watchman with whom you have no previous
relationship. Regardless of how your watchmen come, it is important
to establish a working relationship with them.

One of the hardest things for you as a leader will be to trust the
revelation the watchman is bringing. Remember that you may not
see what they are seeing. This is where it may take blind faith on
your part to trust what the watchman speaks is true. Trust is going
to be one of the major keys in the overall functioning between the
relationship of the leader and the watchman.

When you are in doubt as to what your watchman may be
relaying to you, it is OK for you to ask God for confirmation to
what the watchman is saying. The Word declares that everything
"is established through two or three witnesses". If there is an attack

or something to be alarmed about, God will certainly confirm this to you.

In the next chapter, I will write about what you as a leader can do to help the process of growing an immature watchman into a productive functioning watchman.

---

[1] Rick Joyner, The Perfect Storms, *The Morning Star Prophetic Bulletin,* March 2003. Used by permission. www.morningstarministries.org

Chapter Ten

Leadership's Role and Responsibilities

The role and responsibilities of a watchman were reviewed in chapters two and five. As a leader, if you have not already read those chapters it would be helpful for you to do so. Much of what is written is to help the watchman understand his or her role and act accordingly. However, many leaders do not fully understand the role of the watchman themselves and this information will be useful to them as well.

What Leaders Need to Do

What do you do when you have an immature watchman? Watchmen rarely arrive fully mature; most likely they will be quite new to their gifting and lack understanding themselves. Watchmen are not fully-grown when they begin to see things; oftentimes they are just as puzzled by their gift as you are. When you become aware that you have immature watchmen budding before your eyes, it will become your responsibility to nurture and train these young ones. In order for them to grow in their gifting, they will need the support of their leaders. You will need to pastor and train them in their responsibilities.

An important thing that a leader must understand is that God has appointed these watchmen. Man does not appoint them. It would be great if we could just hand select our watchmen, and then train and deploy them. Unfortunately, we do not get to pick our watchmen, but we do have the obligation before God to train and deploy them.

God is giving them the revelation, and it is your responsibility as a leader to recognize their position as watchmen and help them to mature in this gift.

One of the most important things I can emphasize to you as a leader is that you will need to provide a safe place for these watchmen to exercise their gift. They need to have the ability to learn and to risk in your church or ministry. I realize this is not easy for you as a leader. Babies make messes and the babies are not the ones who generally have to clean up these messes. Often you will be the one who has to clean them up. However, we must remember that we too were once babies. It was likely that someone else was cleaning up our messes while we learned and grew into our leadership position.

In order for watchmen to function properly, he or she will need much grace extended to them from their leaders as they learn to grow in their gifting. It will be worthwhile for you as a leader to invest in the time and training it takes to produce a mature watchman. In the end you will see the blessing of having mature watchmen on the walls of your ministry. With these mature watchmen in their positions, you will find that the enemy is being defeated more often than he gains access and victory over different situations within your ministry.

As you train your watchmen, it is important that they be provided with the policies you have set up concerning how to handle the revelation they have received. Once they understand what is expected of them, it makes it easier for them to be responsible in their role. It is less likely for a person to step over their bounds when the role and expectations have been clearly stated for them.

When an immature watchman messes up, it will be very important for you as a leader to encourage them to try again. Sometimes they will err in how they present their revelation. Oftentimes, they can feel such urgency in their spirit that they try to impose that urgency upon you. You may then want to offer them help on how to present the words the next time they have revelations to bring, rather than scorning them for their immaturity.

They may also err in the understanding of what they have seen or heard. Again, it will be important for you as a leader to encourage them to try again. Whatever messes they make, it is not as though they cannot be fixed. You as a leader will need to have much patience during this training time of your watchmen.

You are the spiritual gatekeeper, their shepherd. I Peter 5:1-4 says:

> *"The elders who are among you I exhort, I who am a fellow elder and a witness of the sufferings of Christ, and also a partaker of the glory that will be revealed;* **Shepherd the flock of God which is among you, serving as overseers, not by compulsion but willingly, not for dishonest gain but eagerly; nor as being lords over those entrusted to you, but being examples to the flock** *and when the Chief Shepherd appears, you will receive the crown of glory that does not fade away."*

As the spiritual gatekeeper, shepherd, pastor, it will be necessary for you to provide protection and oversight of these watchmen. Your watchmen will need to feel your support and protection as they learn to function in their role. Trust not only needs to be felt by the leader to the watchman, but the watchman also needs to feel a level of trust from their leader.

When you have recognized a person to be a watchman and feel they are trustworthy, then it would be good to let them know who the other watchmen are. Each watchman only knows in part. Every piece of revelation is like a piece of a puzzle. When other watchman can come together to discuss their pieces of revelation, a picture begins to form in the puzzle and understanding becomes more clear concerning the revelation.

I suggest that when you have a few good watchmen functioning in their role, that you set up a watchman team. This team should be limited to only those whom you have recognized as watchmen and who are teachable and trainable. This group should meet on a regular basis to discuss and pray about the revelation that God is revealing concerning your ministry. You may want to be the overseer of this ministry at first, but in time you can put someone else in that place, perhaps one of the watchmen who appear to be mature in their gifting as watchman. Whomever you should choose, they will need to be one who is filled with the Holy Spirit and exhibits maturity and wisdom.

Having a watchman team in place will help eliminate a lot of brush fires that you might have had to deal with, and it will free you to only having to deal with the real fires. When a watchman team can be formed, you will find it to be a great help to your ministry. The watchman team can discuss the revelation God has given through dreams and visions or by any other avenue the Lord may have disclosed the revelation. Once the revelation is understood, the watchmen can agree together in prayer and thus have a better understanding of whether or not this particular revelation needs to be reported to the leader. If it is something of a brush fire, they can deal with it in prayer and only report that which is a serious fire. When a true fire is evident, then you can take the information given by the watchmen to your leaders and intercessory team to inquire of the Lord as to the plan of strategy concerning this fire.

As the leader of your ministry, you have the spiritual influence to either permit or rebuke unfortunate dangers that the enemy may send your way. The things you allow in your own life as well as your congregation can bring either blessing or damage to your church or ministry. This is why it is so important that the leader listens to the revelation and warnings the watchmen bring. I am not saying that you must heed every word that comes, but you will need to be responsible to seek God as to whether this word is from Him or not. Spiritually blind or careless ministers are a danger not only to their ministry, but also to the people in their congregations. Ezekiel chapter thirty-four speaks about the irresponsible shepherds. Pastoral pride would say, "If God wanted to warn me of something, He would tell me Himself." This is like saying, "I know it all concerning this ministry and have no need of others to tell me anything; afterall, I am the one God put in charge." As leaders, we must be very careful not to fall into that trap. We have need of one another, and you as a leader have need of watchmen.

The opposite of thinking one has no need of anyone to tell them what the Lord is saying concerning their ministry is the leader hearing the words and disregarding them. One of the greatest dangers in the life of a leader is to be passive in your leading by hiding your head in the sand. This will not make any problems go away, but it can make them worse. If we do not address the warnings the watchmen bring, we can end up with even more problems than we had before the words of warning were given.

It should not surprise you that God might use a watchman to challenge you in your ministry. This is not a negative challenge, but one from God to have you as a leader take a closer look at the problems that might lie within your ministry or church. Be open to what God might be saying to you through your watchmen. It could mean that unfortunate tragedies might be diverted, leaving you with less of a mess to deal with later.

As a leader, you have been given the authority to open or close the gates of your city. This is your God-given task, but even at your best, you cannot see much beyond the walls. Watchmen have the ability to see beyond the walls and discern the dangers that are about to befall the ministry; however, they have limited authority to take the appropriate actions unless a leader is willing to cooperate with the warning. This is why it is so important for the leaders and the watchmen to form an alliance. With the watchmen discerning the potential problems and the leaders exercising their authority, the enemy doesn't stand a chance. With the two working together in unity and through the prayer of agreement, they are able to close the gaps and keep the foxes out!

What Leaders Should Not Do

When watchmen bring you their revelation, they are just doing what God is expecting of them. Ezekiel 33:6 states:

> *"So you, son of man; I have made you a watchman for the house of Israel; therefore you shall hear a word from My mouth and **warn them for Me**."*

Be careful not to take offense or take it personally when the watchman warns you regarding a threat or danger from within. God has exposed something to them, which needs to be prayed through or dealt with. They are just doing their job. God is asking them to warn you for Him.

Dutch Sheets writes in his book called "Watchman Prayer":

"Seasoned watchmen are often alerted by the Holy Spirit before ever having any concrete evidence, that certain messengers are not to be trusted. They recognize wolves sent to devour the flock, or hirelings with improper motives, and bring warnings to those in leadership. Being alerted by their stride – something just doesn't seem right – watchmen sense and discern. To be sure, we must guard against human suspicion and judging after the flesh. But I have learned to listen to my trusted watchmen (one of whom is my wife) when uneasiness prevails about so and so. They are usually right. At times, these watchmen are unable to give me specific reasons, which is difficult for my analytical mind, but I have learned to trust them."

"Many of Satan's activities are 'odorless' – hidden from our natural senses. God has added odorants to the evil one's works, however, that can be discerned by spiritual senses. Hebrews 5:14 tells us, 'But solid food is for the mature, who because of practice have their senses trained to discern good and evil.' Most false doctrine, division and general destruction in the Body of Christ could be averted if the watchmen would exercise these senses and the leaders would listen!" [1]

Dutch Sheets found that his watchmen were able to discern things that were hidden from his natural senses. At times, he declares that it was difficult for his analytical mind to comprehend, but in the end, he learned to trust his watchmen.

Our first response sometimes to a word of warning that we do not see is to become defensive in our position as a leader. The revelation may not seem right to us because we have not yet found it to be true. If we are walking by the sight of our natural senses, then it is likely that we will not be able to receive the revelation. However, God calls us to not walk by the flesh, but to walk by the Spirit. When we as leaders have a conflict in what we are hearing from the watchman versus what we feel we know in the natural, then it becomes necessary for us to ask God to confirm what the watchman has said.

We must be careful that we do not belittle the watchmen or subtly punish them because we do not understand the revelation they are bringing. Most likely, your watchmen have been back and forth before the Lord making sure what they have seen or heard from the Lord is correct. As a watchman, I found it difficult when the Lord would expose something to me. Everything around me seemed to appear the opposite of what God was showing, and it appeared that no other person seemed to be seeing what I was discerning. It made me doubt that I was hearing God. Often I would get caught in this trap and I would have to ask God to confirm to me over and over that what He revealed was true. God was always there to confirm those important warnings, and the accuracy of my reports continued to increase helping me to realize that I had no other choice but to listen to the Spirit of God and walk by His Spirit rather than my natural senses.

As a leader, we must be sure to walk by the Spirit and not by our natural senses. Once we have our confirmations concerning the watchman's revelation, we must proceed to inquire of the Lord as to the handling of these warnings. We cannot ignore issues or put off dealing with them. If we fail to act, we will be forced to deal with them in the future when the stakes are much higher.

Leaders, God is for you. It is His desire for your vision and ministry to become all that it was destined to be. He placed the vision in you that you have for your ministry. In order for your ministry to fulfill all that God desires, it will be necessary for you to recognize the importance of the role of the watchman in your ministry. God is calling His leaders and watchmen to work together in unity and teamwork. It is essential that leaders begin to recognize those who have been placed as watchmen in their ministry, and to begin to train them to become mature in this gift as watchman. As you do these things, you will see the power of God rest in your ministry as never before and will be moving toward what God had destined for you and your ministry in this hour.

---

[1] Dutch Sheets, *Watchman Prayer* (Ventura, CA: Regal Books, 2000), pp. 33-34.

Chapter Eleven

Sheep, Goats and Wolves

Throughout the gospels Jesus often used symbolic language such as parables when speaking to the people. He used figurative speech with illustrations familiar to His audience. One example is when He called certain disciples to come follow Him. In Matthew 4:18-19 we read,

> *And Jesus, walking by the Sea of Galilee, saw two brothers, Simon called Peter, and Andrew his brother, casting a net into the sea; for they were fishermen. Then He said to them, "Follow Me, and I will make you fishers of men."*

Likewise, we find Jesus communicating with terms such as shepherds, sheep, goats, wolves, flocks and herds. Jesus used these terms because an agrarian lifestyle was familiar to His contemporaries. Today, we may not be as familiar with these terms so understanding them can sometimes be difficult. It is my desire to study the characteristics of these animals to better understand Jesus' meaning when using them figuratively.

Much of what I will write has come from the literal and spiritual interpretation from the Bible. I have also gleaned much information from the writers of many articles and books. The information I have found has a common thread amongst them.

Sheep

Sheep are commonly used throughout the Bible to symbolically refer to God's people. We see this in Psalm 95:7:

> *"For He is our God, and we are the people of His pasture, and the sheep of His hand."*

In light of that scripture, let us keep in mind the spiritual application from the scriptures that will be used in this chapter. In Matthew 25, Jesus tells a parable using sheep and the goats.

> *"When the Son of Man comes in His glory, and the holy angels with Him then He will sit on the throne of His glory. All the nations will be gathered before Him, and He will separate them one from another, as a shepherd divides his sheep from the goats. And He will set the sheep on His right hand, but the goats on the left. Then the King will say to those on His right hand, 'Come, you blessed of My Father, inherit the kingdom prepared for you from the foundation of the world'"* (Matthew 25:31-34).

> *"Then He will also say to those on the left hand, 'Depart from Me, you cursed, into the everlasting fire prepared for the devil and his angels'"* (Matthew 25:41).

Although there are similarities between a sheep and goat, there are differences so great that Jesus said the goats would not inherit the kingdom of God. While the sheep are considered God's children, the goats are not. Though, sheep and goats can remain in the same fold, when Jesus returns in all His glory, He will separate the sheep from the goats.

Sheep are gentle, quiet, innocent animals. They do not give their shepherds a lot of problems. If you are having problems with your "sheep" you may find out that you are really looking at a "goat." In

II Samuel 12:3 we read,

> *"But the poor man had nothing, except one little ewe (female) lamb which he had bought and nourished; and it grew up together with him and with his children. It ate of his own food and drank from his own cup and lay in his bosom; and it was like a daughter to him".*

Although this scripture is a parable that Nathan spoke to David when confronting him about his sin with Bathsheba, it reveals that sheep can be affectionate, gentle animals. Not only are they affectionate and gentle, but they can also be considered non-aggressive as seen in the following scriptures:

> *"He was oppressed and He was afflicted, yet He opened not His mouth; He was led as a lamb to the slaughter, and as a sheep before its shearers is silent, so He opened not His mouth"* (Isaiah 53:7).

> *"But I was like a docile lamb brought to the slaughter; and I did not know that they had devised schemes against me, saying, 'Let us destroy the tree with its fruit, and let us cut him off from the land of the living, that his name may be remembered no more'"* (Jeremiah 11:19).

These scriptures show that the lamb or sheep is not aggressive. They are very docile animals. The word "docile" as described in the Webster's dictionary is, "easily managed or handled, readily trained or taught." Even though sheep are easily managed, this does not eliminate the need of care and supervision provided by the shepherd, as noted from the following scriptures.

> *"Who may go out before them and go in before them, who may lead them out and bring them in, that the*

congregation of the Lord may not be like sheep which have no shepherd" (Numbers 27:17).

"So they were scattered because there was no shepherd; and they became food for all the beasts of the field when they were scattered" (Ezekiel 34:5).

"But when He saw the multitudes, He was moved with compassion for them, because they were weary and scattered, like sheep having no shepherd" (Matthew 9:36).

If sheep are not cared for properly, they will become food for all the beasts of the field. After all, sheep are defenseless animals. In Matthew 10:16 we read,

"Behold, I send you out as sheep in the midst of wolves. Therefore be wise as serpents and harmless as doves"

Sheep are not only defenseless, but this scripture would also indicate that sheep are vulnerable to danger, reaffirming their need to be shepherded. Sheep love to follow the shepherd. They feel comfort with the presence of a shepherd. Unfortunately, though, sheep will follow the shepherds even if they are irresponsible as outlined in Ezekiel 34. This is because sheep are very trusting animals and are easily led. However, when sheep are not shepherded properly, they become vulnerable to attack. The attack can come from either outside the fold or from within the flock, since sheep and goats can be found in the same fold.

Sheep are grazers, unlike the goat, which instead likes to browse. The sheep enjoy eating in lush green pastures. In Ezekiel 34:14 it says,

"I will feed them in good pasture, and their fold shall be on the high mountains of Israel. There they shall

*lie down in a good fold and feed in rich pasture on
the mountains of Israel."*

When sheep are fed properly, in lush green pastures, they will also find rest there. They will lie down in those good fields. Lying down is a sign of passivity and submission. When one animal obeys another, this is called submission. You can find two types of submission. One is active and the other is passive. Active submission is when a dominant animal forces another animal to obey it. Passive submission is when a subordinate animal lowers itself to the ground without being forced by the dominant animal. By acting submissive in a fight situation, an animal can avoid serious injury.   The fact that sheep lie down on their own would indicate that they are operating in passive submission. Sheep would rather submit than fight. Being herbivores, sheep do not prey on other animals. They are content in a safe environment and are harmless and unobtrusive. Their demands are simple; they rarely make a noise except to let you know they are hungry or fear danger.

Unfortunately sheep do not always get to eat in lush green pastures. In Ezekiel 34:19 it says,

> *"And for My flock, they eat what you have trampled
> with your feet, and they drink what you have fouled
> with your feet."*

In some situations, where the pastures have not been lush and green or where the shepherds have been irresponsible, God will scatter His sheep. He will bring them out of the fold and lead them into the fold of His choice where they will be able to eat and lie down in green pastures. In Ezekiel 34:13-15 says,

> *"And I will bring them out from the peoples and
> gather them from the countries, and will bring them
> to their own land; I will feed them on the mountains
> of Israel, in the valleys and in all the inhabited places
> of the country. I will feed them in good pasture, and*

> *their fold shall be on the high mountains of Israel.*
> *There they shall lie down in a good fold and feed in*
> *rich pasture on the mountains of Israel. I will feed*
> *My flock and I will make them lie down," says the*
> *Lord God.*

God desires for all of His sheep to feed in good pastures with caring shepherds. In Psalm 23:1-2, David relates himself as a sheep to his shepherd.

> *"The Lord is my shepherd; I shall not want.   He*
> *makes me to lie down in green pastures; He leads me*
> *beside the still waters."*

David is describing his relationship with the Great Shepherd. David himself was a shepherd so he knew very well the behavior of sheep. In this verse, David shares another characteristic about these animals; sheep love still waters. They love peaceful, quiet conditions and to drink from still waters. They are not comfortable with agitated waters. When the waters become agitated, the sheep become skittish.

Now that we have looked at some of the natural tendencies of sheep, let's see how we might apply those natural tendencies to the spiritual application of sheep to the shepherd. We have learned that scripture often refers to sheep as being the children of God and shepherds as pastors or leaders. Flocks or folds represent our congregations. Remember that both sheep and goats can be found in the same flock. Jesus says in Matthew 25 that He will come in all His glory and separate the sheep from the goats suggesting that they had been in the same fold. We find a similar parable or analogy in Matthew 13 where Jesus talks about the wheat and the tares growing up together.

> *"Another parable He put forth to them, saying: 'The*
> *kingdom of heaven is like a man who sowed good*
> *seed in his field; but while men slept, his enemy came*

*and sowed tares among the wheat and went his way.
But when the grain had sprouted and produced a
crop, then the tares also appeared. So the servants
of the owner came and said to him, 'Sir, did you not
sow good seed in your field? How then does it have
tares?' He said to them, 'An enemy has done this.'
The servants said to him, 'Do you want us then to go
and gather them up?' But he said, 'No, lest while you
gather up the tares you also uproot the wheat with
them. Let both grow together until the harvest, and
at the time of harvest I will say to the reapers, 'First
gather together the tares and bind them into bundles
to burn them, but gather the wheat into my barn.'''*

The wheat and the tares are allowed to grow together in the
same field until the time of harvest. At that time, the wheat will be
gathered into the barn (kingdom of God) and the tares will be bound
in bundles to be burned.

Although sheep and goats can dwell together in the same fold, it
is important for leaders to recognize the differences so that the sheep
are not mistaken for goats.

To review, true sheep (God's children) are affectionate and non-
aggressive. They are easy to manage because they are submissive
in nature. They rarely give the shepherd (their leader) problems. If
they should give the shepherd a problem it is generally because the
presence of a wolf or the butting of a goat has agitated them. Also,
sheep enjoy still waters, not liking to drink from agitated waters.
This means that they are not quick to be where strife, arguing,
dissension or turmoil is present. Such problems make the sheep
skittish and they are quick to scurry away from such discord.

Truly, sheep love to graze, meaning they love to eat of the word
of God. They love to be in the presence of God. They rarely will
miss a feeding or shall we say a meeting. They are hungry and love
to graze in green pastures. They are not in a hurry to move on and
will stay as long as the shepherd allows.

Although sheep are easily managed, they also are defenseless and vulnerable to danger. As leaders, it is important to provide the sheep with a comfortable, safe environment. We can do that as leaders if we recognize the danger of allowing wolves into the folds. This will come with the watchman and the leader working together. The watchman will sense the danger of a wolf long before it is able to attack the sheep. Before we see how much danger a wolf can present though, let's take a look at the characteristics of a goat.

Goats

The scripture does not give a lot of indication to the natural tendencies of a goat. What we can find from the scriptures concerning goats is that they were a useful animal. Just like the sheep, goats were allowed to be used as a sacrifice before God as long as they were without spot or blemish. Goats were also considered to be a clean food and could be eaten. Their skin was used to make clothing and the milk was used for food. These would all seem like very good things. However, we do read that the goats will be separated from the sheep when Jesus comes in all His glory. This would indicate that goats are different from sheep. Since the Bible is not clear on some of the characteristics of a goat, I will have to relate information that I found as a consensus amongst those that have raised or tended goats.

Overall, a goat's reputation is less than positive. Even goat metaphors are negative. For instance, "Look at the old goat" refers to an old fool or dirty old man. "You get my goat!" applies to a person who irritates another. The poem, "Mary had a little lamb, its fleece was white as snow; and everywhere that Mary went, the lamb was sure to go" gives such a positive look at a little lamb, but when the gypsy girl Esmeralda in The Hunchback of Notre Dame has a pet goat that performs tricks, the people want to hang the girl because they presume she's using witchcraft. Anyway you look at it; goats tend to be seen in a negative way. Perhaps it is because of the natural tendencies that a goat displays.

Whereas sheep are gentle, quiet and easily led, goats are pushy, self-sufficient and headstrong. Most goats are naturally horned, but many sheep breeds are polled or naturally hornless. Those goat horns can be used to bring harm to another. Also, goats are naturally quarrelsome and have short tempers. They rear and butt in order to establish dominance. Rather than being a passive animal like the sheep, they have more aggressive tendencies.

Goats do not require as much supervision or care as sheep. Perhaps this is because they are a more independent animal. Unlike sheep, goats will easily revert back to their wild conditions if given a chance. Goats do not graze like sheep do, but instead browse. They nibble here and there, sampling a variety of bushes and leaves. Because they are browsers and do not graze, they tend to wander as they eat.

Goats also like the high places, often heading upward. They are not herded as well as sheep because they would rather lead than follow.

Two striking differences between sheep and goats are that goats have an excessively bad odor and their tails are short and held high.

How do these goat characteristics relate spiritually to the shepherd or leader? If a "goat" is part of a fold, you may see some of these characteristics displayed. Goats are often pushy and can cause undercurrents and dissension. Turmoil and agitation are part of their nature. I believe this is because the goat has a dominating and controlling temperament, rather than a passive and submissive one.

Goats tend to be more self-sufficient than sheep, choosing to browse rather than graze in the pasture. They don't enjoy the green pastures in the same way as the sheep. They are not always satisfied with what the shepherd (leader) gives them. They will nibble on the word of God, a little here and a little there, yet they love to be seen in the high places. The goats walk with their tails held high, spiritually indicating pride, and they emit an offensive odor. There is something distinguishing about the goat, and that is the odor or "air" about them.

All this said, it is important to note that goats are not wolves. They will not eat the sheep because they are not the meat eaters that wolves are. They may be agitators and cause some turmoil for the shepherd, but they are not seriously harmful to the sheep. Perhaps that is why Jesus waits until His return to separate the sheep from the goats. The real danger and threat to our flocks and herds is the wolf.

Wolves

Jesus sternly warns us about wolves in Matthew 7:15.

> *"Beware of the false prophets, who come to you in sheep's clothing, but inwardly they are ravenous wolves."*

Jesus compares the false prophet to a wolf. Note that wolves come appearing like sheep. What is it about the "wolves" that made it necessary for Jesus to warn us to look beyond sheeplike similarities to discern the ravenous wolf?

In Acts 20:28-30, Paul also gives a warning.

> *"Therefore take heed to yourselves and to all the flock, among which the Holy Spirit has made you overseers, to shepherd the church of God which He purchased with His own blood. For I know this, that after my departure savage wolves will come in among you, not sparing the flock. Also from among yourselves men will rise up, speaking perverse things, to draw away the disciples after themselves."*

Paul's warning is similar to the one that Jesus gave. Paul is alerting the leaders to take heed because there will be wolves that sneak in amongst them, and they will not spare the flock. These wolves are savage, ravenous animals. They will stop at nothing to devour the flock. This would seem like common knowledge concerning a wolf but in both scriptures the warning is sure that they will come in and may not be recognized as wolves.

Why would we not discern these wolves? The Bible is clear about typical traits wolves' display. Note these scriptures:

> *"Benjamin is **a ravenous wolf**; in the morning **he shall devour the prey**, and at night he shall divide the spoil"* (Genesis 49:27).

> *"Therefore a lion from the forest shall slay them, a*

wolf of the deserts shall destroy them; *a leopard will watch over their cities. Everyone who goes out from there shall be torn in pieces, because their transgressions are many; their backslidings have increased"* (Jeremiah 5:6).

*"Her princes in her midst are like **wolves tearing the prey**, to shed blood, to destroy people and to get dishonest gain"* (Ezekiel 22:27).

*"Their horses also are swifter than leopards, and **more fierce than evening wolves"*** (Habakkuk 1:8).

*"But a hireling, he who is not the shepherd, one who does not own the sheep, sees the wolf coming and leaves the sheep and flees; and **the wolf catches the sheep and scatters them"*** (John 10:12).

From these scriptures we can see that the wolf is fierce and ravenous; it devours, destroys and tears its prey as it scatters and slays sheep. With such vivid descriptions, why would Jesus and Paul need to give us a warning concerning them? One would think that we would be naturally on guard and easily spot a wolf, yet these are warranted warnings from God.

In my research, I discovered attributes about wolves that might cause one to miss the threat of their presence.

The most significant trait of wolves is their intelligence and social behavior. Wolves are friendly, social animals. They learn things quickly and possess a good memory. With keen hearing and a strong sense of smell they can hear or smell your presence long before you might see them.

Wolves are family oriented, living tightly knit in family groups called packs. Wolves mate for life; when a mate dies, the single wolf will seek another mate.

Impressive! Spiritually speaking, these positive traits are how we would like our sheep of the pastures to be! Who wouldn't want smart, charming, sociable sheep that are family-oriented and committed to one mate as part of their congregation? Sounds good, doesn't it? But maybe this is why Jesus warned; "They come to you in sheep's clothing." They look so sweet, innocent and like the perfect little lambs, yet inwardly they are ravenous wolves.

We must remember that wolves are wild, meat eating animals. They devour their prey. They are the ones in our congregations that we need to watch out for. Wolves kill. No one is outside their sphere and can become prey to them. It is important that the leaders recognize and deal with any wolf that may be found in their congregation. An interesting thing to note in regards to wolves is that prey that refuses to run will usually survive a wolf attack. When prey stands its ground, the wolves surround the animal and lie down. We must not fear the wolf or possible attack, but take a stand against it so that our churches and congregations will not suffer the damage a wolf can do.

Jesus referred to these wolves as "false prophets." They look like sheep, may even sound like sheep, but inwardly they are ravenous. How do we recognize them? How do we see past the social, charming, talented animals to know that they are falsely represented?

The major way we will discern the wolves is through our watchmen. The watchmen are given the ability to "see" beyond what is seen in the natural to what is spiritual. The watchmen are the ones who will recognize that there is a zipper that unfolds the sheep costume to reveal the wolf residing inside. They are able to see the "inward part" that is not evident to the natural eye but is given through the Spirit of God. God will reveal to His watchmen the inner wolf characteristics that devour the prey.

Sheepdogs

While researching sheep and goats I felt inspired to study sheepdogs. Interestingly, Sheepdogs parallel the role of a watchman. As you read these natural tendencies of the sheepdog, keep in mind the watchman and his role.

There are two types of sheepdogs, herding dogs and guarding

dogs. Herding dog's work primarily by moving sheep from one area to another by biting, chasing, or barking at the sheep. This is not the type of sheepdog that our watchmen are to emulate. Instead, the watchmen are to resemble the guarding dog. Guarding dogs do not herd sheep; they are discouraged from biting, chasing, and barking at the sheep, but rather have protective behaviors that sense intruders, and their bark is heard when a predator has been spotted.

Sheepdogs were used for centuries to partner with the shepherds. These guard dogs become a full-time member of the flock. They will investigate intruders and alert the shepherd of any potential danger. The success of the dog is a result of proper rearing. The guarding sheepdog is an essential "tool" to be incorporated into the overall management of a sheep operation.

The primary mission of a sheepdog is to guard and protect the herds against predators (wild animals or thieves). These guard dogs have become very effective in controlling predators while remaining very caring and gentle towards children. Most guard dogs are intelligent, alert and confident. The dogs alert the shepherds to disturbances (predators) near the flock, which help to reduce the predator problems. This brings protection for the family members and farm property by alerting the shepherd to potential problems.

As you can see from the benefits listed above, it would be in the best interest of a shepherd (leader) to employ the help of sheepdogs (watchmen) to keep watch over their flocks (congregations). This will help in the reduction of predator problems, along with bringing a peace of mind to the shepherd that his flock is doing well and that he will be alerted to any problem that may arise.

Shepherds

The Bible teaches that Jesus Christ is our Shepherd and we are the sheep of His pasture. Jesus is our perfect example of what it is to be a shepherd, making it our responsibility to learn to be a good shepherd.

The basic functions of a shepherd are to provide food and water, protection and healing. The feeding of the sheep is the most important responsibility of the shepherd. An example of the importance of feeding the sheep can be found in John 21:15-17,

> *"So when they had eaten breakfast, Jesus said to*
> *Simon Peter, 'Simon, son of Jonah, do you love Me*
> *more than these?' He said to Him, 'Yes, Lord; You*
> *know that I love you.' He said to him, 'Feed My lambs.'*
> *He said to him again a second time, 'Simon, son of*
> *Jonah, do you love Me?' He said to Him, 'Tend My*
> *sheep.' He said to him the third time, 'Simon, son of*
> *Jonah, do you love me?' Peter was grieved because*
> *He said to him the third time; 'Do you love Me?' And*
> *he said to Him, 'Lord, You know all things; you know*
> *that I love you.' Jesus said to him, 'Feed My sheep.'"*

Jesus was emphatic about having His flock fed. As good shepherds we are required to nourish the flock. The shepherd needs to consider the needs of his sheep and provide the food that will have the most nutritional advantage to the animal.

Along with providing food for the sheep, the shepherd must also provide water. As we learned earlier, sheep enjoy still waters, making it the responsibility of the shepherd to provide a safe environment for the sheep to graze and be refreshed. Remember that sheep become skittish when the waters are agitated or stirred. It is important that the shepherd lead his sheep to still waters in order to drink.

One of the greatest tasks of the shepherd is the protection of the flock. David was a shepherd of the sheep and he knew the importance of protecting the flock. In the story of David and Goliath, note that David was accustomed to fighting for and protecting the sheep. I Samuel 17:32-36 says,

> *"Then David said to Saul, 'Let no man's heart fail*
> *because of him; your servant will go and fight with*
> *this Philistine.' And Saul said to David, 'You are not*
> *able to go against this Philistine to fight with him; for*
> *you are a youth, and he a man of war from his youth.'*
> *But David said to Saul, 'Your servant used to keep his*

*father's sheep, and when a lion or a bear came and
took a lamb out of his flock, I went out after it and
struck it, and delivered the lamb from its mouth; and
when it arose against me, I caught it by its beard, and
struck and killed it. Your servant has killed both the
lion and bear; and this uncircumcised Philistine will
be like one of them, seeing he has defied the armies
of the living God.'"*

In days past, shepherds relied on sheepdogs to help protect the
flock. When the sheepdog alerted the shepherd to predators, the
shepherd needed to fight the devourer and rescue the sheep.

Today, the shepherds may employ more modern means of
protecting the fold. They may use electric fencing, spotlights
and cameras to check on the animals at night, alerting them to
any intruders. Our watchmen, given the opportunity, can become
the modern technologies use to spot predators. They can become
the spotlights and cameras at night to alert the shepherds of any
intruders. All they need is the support and training to help them
become mature in their gifting as watchmen.

Lastly, a shepherd is required to care for the sick and lame sheep
and provide healing. Even with all the modern conviences one
might use to watch and protect the sheep, one is still required to
examine the animals each day for the sick and lame. In the past
shepherds had to fulfill the role of our veterinarians today. They
had the responsibility to apply balm, olive oil or animal fat used
as an ointment to the injuries of the animal. Today, our shepherds
(leaders) must do the same and provide the medical help through
the healing balm of Jesus Christ. It may be necessary to provide
teachings on inner healing and deliverance (surgery) to see the
complete manifested healing for the sheep.

As far as the responsibilities of a shepherd to the sheepdog, a
leader must provide a safe environment for the growth of the animal.
Just as sheepdogs are puppies to start out with and the shepherd has
need of training and rearing them as they grow and mature, we as
leaders need to recognize the puppy watchmen in our flocks and train

and equip them. The goal with a new sheep dog puppy is to channel its natural instincts to produce a mature guardian dog. So must we channel the watchman's natural instincts to produce a mature sheep dog that will be a blessing to our leaders and in our congregations. If leaders do this, they will find loyal lifetime sheepdogs that will help protect the flock they are entrusted with.

Chapter Twelve

Backlash

As anointed men and women of God move into what God is calling them to do, they begin to pose a great threat to the enemy. If we do nothing as Christians, then Satan has nothing to fear. His kingdom is not threatened. However, once we step into the anointing which God calls us to, then we become a threat to our enemy and to his kingdom. At this point, the powers of hell are unleashed upon us to keep us from moving forward in our calling. This is not something we should fear, but it is something we should be aware of and must prepare ourselves for.

What is Backlash?

Backlash could be described as an attack from the enemy after a given victory. Webster's dictionary defines backlash as "a sudden, forceful backward movement; recoil." Recoil as defined in Webster's dictionary is "to spring or fly back, as in consequence of force of impact or of a discharge of ammunition." When I read this definition, I began to envision our enemy as that of the serpent. I can picture him recoiling after he receives a force of impact from us as believers. When a serpent recoils, it is now in position to make a quick lash out to strike back at its target.

A second definition of backlash from Webster's is, "a strong negative reaction, as to some social or political change." When the enemy's kingdom is threatened or he experiences some defeat, Satan has a strong negative reaction, which can come in the form of backlash.

The greater the risk we are to the enemy's camp, the greater our fight will be. Satan is always on the attack towards those who pose a threat to his kingdom. His tactics have always been the same. He will usually start out by trying to thwart the work in its beginning. If he does not succeed in thwarting the work through his initial attacks, he will return and try to attack again in the midst of your work. Many times he is successful in his attempts during these early and mid-stages of our ministries by wearing us down through warfare. However, if he cannot gain total victory during those times, he will come after us during one of our most victorious times in the Spirit.

The enemy knows that after we experience a victory, that is the most vulnerable time for us. It does not appear to be a vulnerable time because we are generally on such a high from our recent victory. But what happens is that we let our guards down after the victory, presuming we have won our warfare, and that leaves us wide open for the enemy to attack. While we are celebrating our victory, he is recoiling and getting ready to unleash his attack once again on us. Unfortunately, we are generally not prepared for this attack and the sting of his bite can leave us disabled.

Let us take a look at the story of Elijah in I Kings chapters 18 and 19. In these passages we read about Elijah, a mighty man of God, and how much of a threat he was to King Ahab's kingdom. King Ahab was the reigning king of Israel at this time. Ahab did evil in the sight of the Lord, more than all that were before him. He took as his wife, Jezebel, the daughter of Ethbaal, king of the Sidonians and he served Baal and worshiped him. Ahab and Jezebel were both at war with Elijah, even to the point that Ahab was seeking to kill Elijah. When Obadiah, who was in charge of Ahab's house, found Elijah, he said,

> *"As the Lord your God lives, **there is no nation or kingdom where my master has not sent someone to hunt for you;** and when they said, he is not here, he took an oath from the kingdom or nation that they could not find you" (I Kings 18:10).*

Ahab knew that Elijah posed a threat to his kingdom, which is why Ahab despised Elijah. When Elijah presented himself before Ahab at the Lord's command, Ahab revealed his heart:

> *"Then it happened, when Ahab saw Elijah, that Ahab said to him, 'Is that you, **O troubler of Israel**?'"* (I Kings 18:17).

Ahab considered Elijah to be a troublemaker--and he was! He was trouble to Ahab's kingdom. Elijah stood for righteousness in the face of a compromising Israel. God moved powerfully through him in miracles, signs and wonders. Elijah went after the evil in the house of Israel and killed the false prophets. Elijah was trouble for Ahab and he brought much damage to Ahab's wicked kingdom.

At his meeting with Ahab, Elijah told Ahab to call the 450 prophets of Baal and the 400 prophets of Asherah, along with all of Israel, to Mount Carmel in order to prove who was the true God. They all gathered on Mount Carmel, where Elijah instructed the false prophets to build an altar to their god but to put no fire under it. Elijah did the same and built an altar to the God of Israel, putting no fire under it. Elijah exhorted the people that they should quit faltering between two opinions. He went on to say, "If the Lord is God, follow Him; but if Baal, follow him." Then he told the false prophets to call on the name of their god and he would call on the name of the Lord and whichever God answered by fire, He is the one true God. This seemed agreeable to all the people and thus they did.

The prophets of Baal called out to their god to hear them. Throughout the day they tried many things to get the attention of their gods, yet to no avail. They leaped about their altar hoping for a response of fire, but there was no answer. They even cut themselves with knives and lances until blood gushed out on them. But there was still no answer. (It is amazing to me what people will do to try to prove that the god they believe in is real. I thank God that He doesn't require us to cut ourselves until our blood gushes out. Jesus shed His blood so that we do not have to shed any.)

Elijah mocked the false prophets saying that maybe their god was meditating or busy, on a journey or even sleeping with need of being awakened! Later in the afternoon when there appeared to be no activity from the god of the prophets of Baal, Elijah told everyone to come near to him. He prepared an altar before the Lord, dug a trench around it, put the wood in order and the bull sacrifice upon the altar. Next he poured pots of water over the sacrifice and the wood. He did this three times in order to make sure that the wood and the sacrifice were saturated with water, making it difficult for a fire to start. He wanted to make sure there was no doubt in anyone's mind that the fire was not made by anyone except the Lord God. Then Elijah came near the altar at the evening sacrifice and called upon the Lord. I Kings 18:36-38 says:

> *And it came to pass, at the time of the offering of the evening sacrifice, that Elijah the prophet came near and said, "Lord God of Abraham, Isaac, and Israel,* **let it be known this day that You are God** *in Israel and I am Your servant, and that I have done all these things at your word. Hear me, O Lord, hear me,* **that this people may know that You are the Lord God, and that You have turned their hearts back to You again.**" *Then the fire of the Lord fell and consumed the burnt sacrifice, and the wood and the stones and the dust, and it licked up the water that was in the trench.*

The fire consumed the burnt sacrifice proving that the God which Elijah served was the one and only true God. It didn't take long for the people of Israel to fall on their faces and shout, "The Lord, He is God! The Lord, He is God!" At this point Elijah had the Israelites seize the prophets of Baal. Not one escaped and Elijah executed them all at the Brook Kishon, which means ensnarer. Elijah executed the false prophets at the place which was called "ensnarer." So much for the enemy who ensnared all of Israel to follow false gods! The enemy was defeated and once again, Israel was turned back to serve the God of Israel.

Elijah's ministry was to turn the hearts of the people back to God. He had a great victory that day on Mount Carmel, which means, "fruitful field". He witnessed much fruit on top of that mountain. Certainly he was rejoicing with all of Israel upon that victory.

Following this victory though, was backlash. Most likely, this great prophet of God was not prepared for what happened next.

> *"And Ahab told Jezebel all that Elijah had done, also how he had executed all the prophets with the sword. Then Jezebel sent a messenger to Elijah, saying, 'So let the gods do to me, and more also, if I do not make your life as the life of one of them by tomorrow about this time.' And when he saw that, he arose and ran for his life, and went to Beersheba, which belongs to Judah and left his servant there"* (I Kings 19:1-3).

What happened? Here was this great prophet of God who faced 850 false prophets and executed them all and now he's running for his life at the threat of one woman! How does something like this happen? He had just proven that His God was the one true God and that the gods the false prophets were serving had no power at all, not even enough power to rain down fire upon their altars. Jezebel's threat to Elijah was substantiated by her saying, "I am willing to have the gods I serve kill me, if I don't kill you by tomorrow at this time." What gods? Elijah knew that her gods could not even compare to the God he served. Yet Elijah became very depressed, was frightened and ran for his life.

How could someone like Elijah be overflowing with faith and courage one day, and lack all of it the next? I believe this was because of the spiritual battle that was taking place while Elijah was celebrating his victory. Unaware of the enemy's scheme, Elijah fell prey to backlash. Elijah was not prepared to hear Jezebel's threat. It hit him like a serpents bite because his guard had been let down after his great victory. He was vulnerable for this attack. The enemy had recoiled and now backlashed at Elijah.

Jezebel

We must also look at Jezebel to understand some of the spiritual significance that caused Elijah to experience the depression, fear and defeat. Jezebel was a very strong and influential woman. She did not serve the Lord God but served the god of Baal. She raised up the false prophets of Baal and of Asherah. It was her influence that caused her husband, King Ahab, to walk away from serving the Lord God which resulted in Israel serving other gods.

Jezebel was a woman of power. She held a position of power because she was born into royalty; after all, she was the daughter of Ethbaal, the king of the Sidonians. Jezebel was manipulative and accustomed to getting her way. She would stop at nothing in order to get what she wanted.

I Kings chapter 21, talks about Ahab desiring a vineyard next to his palace that was owned by Naboth the Jezreelite. When Ahab asked Naboth about giving the vineyard to him so that he could have it for a vegetable garden, Naboth refused. This displeased Ahab. Because of Naboth's refusal, Ahab became depressed to the point that he would not even get up from his bed or eat food. Jezebel his wife asked Ahab about his despondency. When Ahab told her it was because Naboth would not give his vineyard to him, Jezebel set out to acquire the vineyard.

Jezebel wrote letters in Ahab's name, put his seal upon them and sent the letters to the elders and nobles of the city. The letters said:

> *Proclaim a fast, and seat Naboth with high honor among the people; and seat two men, scoundrels, before him to bear witness against him, saying, "You have blasphemed God and the king" Then take him out and stone him, that he may die (I Kings 21:9-10).*

Jezebel's unscrupulous activity brought false accusations against Naboth resulting in his death. But Naboth's death was not the only death that Jezebel orchestrated. She was a murderous woman; probably the most wicked of all her crimes was her slaughter of the true prophets of Israel. I Kings 18:4 says:

> *For so it was, while **Jezebel massacred the prophets
> of the Lord** that Obadiah had taken one hundred
> prophets and hidden them, fifty to a cave, and had
> fed them with bread and water.*

Jezebel was determined to exterminate the true prophetic
ministry. So it was in her threat against Elijah, the true prophet
of God. The "spirit of Jezebel" is still trying to kill the prophetic
ministry today.

We can see at war the prophetic spirit of Elijah and evil spirit
Jezebel not only in I Kings, but also in the New Testament account
of John the Baptist and Heriodias (Mark 6:14-29).

In this account, King Herod had bound and jailed John the
Baptist because John had confronted Herod about his relationship
with Herodias, his brother Philip's wife. King Herod had married
Herodias prompting John to declare, "It is not lawful for you to have
your brother's wife."

This of course made Herodias very angry and in her bitterness
she wanted John the Baptist killed. But Herod feared John, knowing
that he was a just and holy man, and even protected him, making
Herodias unwilling to kill the prophet. That is, until an opportune
time presented itself.

On the day of Herod's birthday, he gave a feast for his nobles,
the high officers and the chief men of Galilee. Herodias's daughter
was part of the scheduled entertainment. She danced before the
king and all his party guests, so delighting Herod and those who
sat with him that the king swore to the girl, "Ask me whatever you
want and I will give it to you," up to half his kingdom. The girl
asked her mother what she should request. One would expect the
mother spend some time thinking about her choices, but because
Herodias hated what John the Baptist stood for, she chose to ask
for the head of John the Baptist. She told her daughter that this is
what she should ask for. Immediately the girl went to the king and
requested for John the Baptist's head on a platter. Although the king

was exceedingly sorry for what he had offered the girl, he could not back out because of the oath he took before those who sat with him. The king sent an executioner and commanded John's head to be brought. John was executed that day in prison and his head was brought to the girl on a platter and she in turn gave it to her mother.

We can see from this story how the Jezebel spirit was at work in the life of Herodias. Herodias became angry when confronted by her unrighteous deed of adultery with her husband's brother.

> *Therefore Herodias held it against him and wanted to kill him, but she could not (Matthew 6:19).*

Just as Jezebel was confronted concerning the false prophets and wanted to have Elijah killed, Herodias wanted John the Baptist killed. This confrontation happened in the natural, but that is not the only realm of confrontation. There was a confrontation in the spiritual in which all the forces of hell were hurled towards the act of the righteous one (John the Baptist) resulting in an attack by the spirit of Jezebel through Herodias.

John the Baptist's ministry was to prepare the way of the Lord and to call the people to repentance. Matthew 3:1-3 says:

> *In those days John the Baptist came preaching in the wilderness of Judea, and saying, "Repent for the kingdom of heaven is at hand!" For this is he who was spoken of by the prophet Isaiah, saying: "The voice of one crying in the wilderness: Prepare the way of the Lord; Make His paths straight."*

Malachi 4:5-6 says:

> *"Behold, I will send you Elijah the prophet before the coming of the great and dreadful day of the Lord and he will turn the hearts of the fathers to the children, and the hearts of the children to their fathers, lest I come and strike the earth with a curse."*

Jesus said in Matthew 11:14 concerning John the Baptist:

"And if you are willing to receive it, he is Elijah who is to come."

This verse does not mean that John the Baptist was the reincarnated Elijah, but it is revealing that the spirit of Elijah was resting upon John the Baptist. The same anointing was on John because he had the same life commission, namely, to turn the hearts of the people back to God.

If you are involved in a ministry of reconciliation, a ministry that wants to see the hearts of the people return to God, and if you are preaching the uncompromising Word, then you will also be a target for the Jezebel spirit to attack your ministry. Or if you are a cutting-edge true prophetic ministry, this too will cause you to become a target for the spirit of Jezebel. Just as Jezebel hated Elijah and what he stood for and wanted him dead, and just as Herodias hated John the Baptist and wanted him killed, the spirit of Jezebel hates you and wants to kill your ministry.

We cannot remain ignorant of the enemy's schemes. The Jezebel spirit is real and alive and working against ministries today. This spirit has taken out many a good ministry. It is the watchmen who are able to discern the workings of a Jezebel spirit. Without the watchmen in place, Jezebel goes unseen and finds an opportune time to take down a minister or even an entire ministry. This spirit will stop at nothing to kill the true prophetic ministries that are in operation today.

Unfortunately, Jezebel has been able to work her way in our ministries and she is not easily detected. Jezebel knows our language and sounds just like one of us. Satan knows God and he has counterfeited Him to where many people have been deceived. If it were always easy to tell the difference between the holy and the unholy when it comes to the prophetic, we would not be having the problems we do today with the prophetic ministry. The same was true with the prophets of old. Many people were deceived because they could not distinguish between the true prophetic and the false.

The prophets of old were prophesying peace to Israel when God was not speaking peace. In Jeremiah 23:21-22 it says:

> *"I have not sent these prophets, yet they ran. I have not spoken to them yet they prophesied. But if they had stood in My counsel, and had caused My people to hear My words, then they would have turned them from their evil way and from the evil of their doings."*

Jeremiah seemed to be the only prophet who was speaking of the coming bondage of Israel. The words he spoke were not what the majority of the prophets were speaking. Many believed Jeremiah to be the false prophet of their time. Yet he was speaking the true prophetic voice of the Lord.

There is another time when just one prophet was speaking something different from all the other prophets, as noted in I Kings 22. In this passage, Jehoshaphat, the king of Judah, visits Ahab, the king of Israel. The king of Israel asks King Jehoshaphat if he would go with him to fight at Ramoth Gilead. Jehoshaphat responds to the king of Israel, "I am as you are, my people as your people, my horses as your horses." But King Jehoshaphat feels it is necessary to inquire of the prophets for the word of the Lord. So the king of Israel gathers the prophets together, about 400 men, and asks, "Shall I go against Ramoth Gilead to fight, or shall I refrain?" They advise him "to go up for the Lord will deliver Ramoth Gilead into the hand of the king." For some reason, this does not seem valid to King Jehoshaphat. So Jehoshapaht asks, "Is there not still a prophet of the Lord here, that we may inquire of Him?"

Four hundred prophets had just declared that they should go and fight and that God would deliver the enemy into the hand of the king. Why on earth would King Jehoshaphat question them? I believe it was because Jehoshaphat had a "check in his spirit" about the words of these prophets. Having four hundred prophets say the same thing might make you question your discernment. But Jehoshaphat must have felt strongly about this to ask for one more prophet's opinion!

The king of Israel tells Jehoshaphat that there is one other man, Micaiah the son of Imiah, by whom they may inquire of the Lord. He admits to Jehoshaphat the he hates him, because he does not prophesy good concerning the king, but evil.   This appalls King Jehoshaphat who replies, "Let not the king say such things!"

The king calls for Micaiah and an officer is sent in order to bring the prophet to the king.   The officer tells Micaiah, "Now listen, the words of the prophets with one accord encourage the king. Please, let your word be like the word of one of them, and speak encouragement."   Michaiah replies, "As the Lord lives, whatever the Lord says to me that I will speak."   Michaiah goes before the king who asks whether they should war against Ramoth Gilead? Machaiah answers, "Go and prosper, for the Lord will deliver it into the hand of the king!"

Though these were the words that the king of Israel hoped to hear, instead of being pleased he demands, "How many times shall I make you swear that you tell me nothing but the truth in the name of the Lord?" Perhaps Michaiah was being obviously sarcastic with his first response, or maybe the king of Israel expected a negative report, at any rate, the king wanted to hear more from Michaiah.

So Michaiah speaks frankly, telling the king that he sees all Israel scattered on a mountain as sheep that have no shepherd. He reports that the Lord said; "These have no master.   Let each return to his house in peace."   At this point, the king of Israel turns to Jehoshaphat, saying, "Did I not tell you he would not prophesy good concerning me, but evil?" Michaiah's response is in I Kings 22:19-23:

> *"Therefore hear the word of the Lord: I saw the Lord sitting on His throne, and all the host of heaven standing by, on His right hand and on His left. And the Lord said, 'Who will persuade Ahab to go up, that he may fall at Ramoth Gilead?' So one spoke in this manner and another spoke in that manner. Then a spirit came forward and stood before the Lord, and said, 'I will persuade him.' The Lord said to him 'In*

> *what way?' So he said, ' I will go out and be a lying*
> *spirit in the mouth of all his prophets.' And the Lord*
> *said, 'You shall persuade him, and also prevail. Go*
> *out and do so.' Therefore look! The Lord has put a*
> *lying spirit in the mouth of all these prophets of yours,*
> *and the Lord has declared disaster against you."*

Here lies the reason (no pun intended!) why all 400 prophets were speaking falsely: God had allowed a lying spirit to speak from their mouths.

Next came an assault from one of the other prophets, Zedekiah, who struck Micaiah on the cheek, saying, "Which way did the spirit from the Lord go from me to speak to you?" Micaiah responds, "Indeed, you shall see on that day when you go into an inner chamber to hide!"

The king of Israel had Micaiah taken out of his presence and imprisoned, with the orders, "Put this fellow into prison and feed him with the bread of affliction and water of affliction, until he (King Ahab) would come in peace." But Micaiah declares, "If you ever return in peace, the Lord has not spoken by me," and finally warns, "Take heed, all you people!"

Of course, the story ends with the death of Ahab, king of Israel and Micaiah's word proving to be true. Again, we witness one man speak the true word of the Lord while so many other prophetic voices were speaking just the opposite. Sadly, this same problem occurs today. We have prophetic voices declaring just the opposite of one other. I cannot say this is because they are speaking by a lying spirit, but I do believe many may be speaking from their soul realm. They say what they themselves want to hear or believe the people want to hear.

How is one to know the true prophetic voice of the Lord? I believe that in the last days it will become increasingly more difficult for us to know. Our spirit must bear witness with the Spirit of God concerning the prophetic words. But this can only happen if we have an intimate relationship with God. It is through intimacy with Him that we will be able to discern whether the prophetic voice is from Him or whether it is a false prophetic voice.

The false voices in these two references "sounded good" but they were not from God. Jezebel can also sound good. Since she "knows the language," it becomes increasingly difficult to discern when the spirit of Jezebel is operating.

The Jezebel spirit works through people. Often these people are well-meaning Christians who generally have been severely wounded and have need of much healing and deliverance. It is important for us to remember that the people the spirit of Jezebel is working through are victims. Whenever we are dealing with a Jezebel spirit (and we will have them) we must take care to separate the person for which the spirit is operating from the spirit itself. Ephesians 6:12 reminds us:

> *"For we do not wrestle against flesh and blood, but against principalities, against powers, against the rulers of the darkness of this age, against spiritual hosts of wickedness in the heavenly places."*

This is why we are exhorted to put on the whole armor of God: that we may be able to stand against the wiles of the devil. Our warfare should not be against the person in whom the Jezebel spirit is operating, but against the spirit. We need to wage our war against the spirit of Jezebel while continually remembering that the person is the victim of her spirit.

Witchcraft

Many of Jezebel's attacks will come in the form of witchcraft. Witchcraft can be difficult to detect unless we are aware of its effects. Rick Joyner wrote a booklet called "Overcoming Witchcraft," as part of his Combating Spiritual Strongholds Series. This work is packed full of wonderful teaching and wisdom concerning overcoming witchcraft. Joyner answers the question, "What is Witchcraft?" as follows:

> *Witchcraft is counterfeit spiritual authority; it is using a spirit other than the Holy Spirit to dominate,*

*manipulate or control others. In Galatians 5:20
the apostle Paul named witchcraft, or "sorcery,"
as one of the deeds of the flesh. Though witchcraft
has its origin in the carnal nature of man, it usually
degenerates quickly into demonic power. When we
try to use emotional pressure to manipulate others,
it is a basic form of witchcraft. When we use hype
or soul power to enlist service, even for the work of
God, it is witchcraft.* [1]

Rick also says:

*"Because witchcraft is basically rooted in the fear of
man,* **and "the fear of man brings a snare" (Proverbs
29:25)**, *those who begin to operate in witchcraft
are trapped – fear has snared them. The bigger the
project or ministry that we have built with hype,
manipulation or control spirits, the more we will fear
anyone or anything that we cannot manipulate or
control. Those who are caught in this deadly trap
will most fear those who walk in the true anointing
and authority."* [2]

Rick also writes about some other forms of witchcraft, which he
calls, "charismatic witchcraft." Often when we think of witchcraft,
we picture black magic coming from witches and warlocks. That
can be a genuine form of witchcraft, but there is even a subtle form
of witchcraft that comes from within the church. I had never really
contemplated this type of witchcraft until I read the following
excerpts which made much sense.

*The source of the witchcraft used against us may not
be the obvious satanic cults or New Age operatives.
It can come from well-meaning, though deceived,
Christians who are, in effect, praying against us
instead of for us. These misguided prayers have*

*power, because whatever is released on earth is released in heaven, and whatever is bound on earth is bound in heaven. **If intercession is motivated by a spirit of control or manipulation, it is witchcraft, and its power is just as real as that of black magic.***

Other sources of charismatic witchcraft can be such things as gossip, political maneuvering, and jealousy, and they can have an effect on us whether we allow ourselves to be manipulated by them or not. For example, consider the result if we refuse to be manipulated by someone who has a control spirit, but allow ourselves to become resentful or bitter toward that person. In such a case, the enemy has still caused us to fall and the same discouragement, disorientation and depression will come upon us just as surely as if we had submitted to the control spirit. [3]

It was amazing to me to first read that manipulation in prayer could be witchcraft. How many times have we heard someone pray a manipulative prayer rather than the will of God? People mean well by these prayers, but in actuality they are prayers of witchcraft that can affect the people we are praying for.

Oftentimes, when we do not understand a situation we can pray a manipulative prayer instead of by the Spirit of God. For example, let's say that God has moved a person into a church to use him or her in leadership. The leaders recognize the anointing and agree that God has called this person to come alongside and help them.

The decision may not have been made by congregational vote but the leaders, being led by God, have placed this person into a form of leadership. Sometimes in a situation like this, jealousy can arise from among those who have either been in leadership or feel they should be. Jealousy can cause them to feel like their positions are being threatened. Because these people do not understand why this person has been placed in the new role of responsibility, they begin to think that the person wants to take over the ministry, and they see this person as a threat to them and the ministry. When it comes time to pray, their misunderstanding of the situation can cause them to pray manipulatively. They may pray something like this: "Lord, this new person has come in and is trying to take over the church and make changes that are not of you. Help the leaders to see their mistake and please remove them from this role and put someone who has been with us in their place."

This kind of prayer is very manipulative and just as Rick Joyner has written, "these misguided prayers have power, because whatever is released on earth is released in heaven, and whatever is bound on earth is bound in heaven." I believe that if we are not praying according to God's will, then Satan has the opportunity to try to answer our requests. In a situation like the one mentioned above, I believe the enemy begins to unleash confusion, not only against the person who was placed in the ministry by God, but confusion also begins to affect the leaders.

Witchcraft can have many negative effects. Rick Joyner also shares in his book about the attacks of witchcraft and the effects it will have on us. We must be able to discern the effects of witchcraft if we are going to be able to combat it. Below is what Rick says concerning the stings of witchcraft.

The attacks of witchcraft come in a series of stings. The successive stings are meant to hit the very places where we have been weakened by the previous stings. In this way, they build upon each other until the cumulative effect overwhelms the target. The stings of witchcraft usually come in the following order:

- *Discouragement*
- *Confusion*
- *Depression*
- *Loss of Vision*
- *Disorientation*
- *Withdrawal*
- *Despair*
- *Defeat* [4]

Rick takes each one of these stings and breaks them down for us in his book. I am going to relate a portion of each sting here as Rick has written. These portions are not in their entirety, so I would suggest you purchase a copy of this valuable book in order to get the full extent of what Rick is saying.

Sting 1 – Discouragement

Everyone gets discouraged at times and it can be for many different reasons so this is not always the result of witchcraft being used against us. But if we become subject to increasing discouragement for no apparent reason, witchcraft should be considered as a possible source. When your difficulties seem insurmountable and you want to give up, even though matters are really not any worse than usual, you are probably coming under spiritual attack.

Sting 2 – Confusion

Again, we must look for a general and increasing "spirit of confusion" for which there is no apparent reason. Here we begin to lose our clarity as to what we have been called to do, which of course will weaken our resolve.

Sting 3 – Depression

This is a deeper problem than simple discouragement. It is an unshakable dread that comes as a result of the combined effect of discouragement and confusion, along with a general negligence in spiritual disciplines that has usually slipped in by this time.

Sting 4 – Loss of Vision

This is the goal of the previous stings and it works to increase their effect. Here we begin to doubt that God has called us to the task in the first place.

Sting 5 – Disorientation

The combined result of depression, confusion and loss of vision is usually disorientation. By this time, not only have we forgotten the course we are supposed to be holding, but we have even lost our ability to read the compass. The Scriptures will no longer speak to us, and it is a struggle to trust the Lord's voice or receive much encouragement from even the most anointed teaching or preaching.

Sting 6 – Withdrawal

When disorientation sets in, it is tempting to withdraw or retreat from our purpose in the ministry, our fellowship with the rest of the church, and often from our families and others we are close to.

Sting 7 – Despair

Withdrawal from the battle leads quickly to hopelessness and despair. Without hope we can easily be taken out by the enemy, either through temptation, sickness or death.

Sting 8 – Defeat

The enemy's purpose is to weaken us so that we begin to fall farther and farther behind; then we can be picked off more easily. [5]

This information has been a valuable tool for me. When I find myself falling into discouragement and some of these other stings, I am quickly reminded that I may be experiencing the stings of witchcraft. Sometimes it takes awhile before I realize what is happening, but once I do take authority over it, the symptoms begin to decrease. Occasionally, it has progressed to the point that I have needed someone else to pray with me concerning the effects of witchcraft in order to get a breakthrough.

If you are experiencing the stings of witchcraft, take authority in the name of Jesus over the witchcraft "for no weapon formed against you shall prosper and any tongue that rises up against you, you shall condemn" (Is. 54:17). Condemn the words that have been spoken against you, not the person or persons. If this does not seem to lift the symptoms, then by all means, go to someone who can help you break the power of witchcraft over you.

There are times when I enter a meeting and know that there is a form of witchcraft being released in the place. I don't always know if it is against me, the leaders, or the meeting. I generally get a physical sign of this warning. These symptoms will come upon me without any warning. At times when the witchcraft is especially strong, I can get a headache that feels like a vice has been placed around my head. I didn't have it before I stepped into the meeting. Oftentimes it will happen while I am in the intercessory prayer group that meets before the meeting. At other times, I may feel nausea or occasionally dizziness, especially when I am the one scheduled to speak. When this happens, I first pray concerning the witchcraft and opposition that is trying to come against us, but I also notify the leaders and intercessors to pray. Generally I find relief from the symptoms and I am able to minister effectively. I believe that when the symptoms are relieved, it is because the power of witchcraft has been broken.

Sometimes when you experience these types of things, you wonder if anyone else has ever experienced them. There really isn't any frame of reference for this type of attack. I believe it was the Holy Spirit who helped me to understand what was happening to me when these symptoms would occur. It was a delight to me when I found out that I was not the only person that would receive physical warnings alerting me to witchcraft. (I wasn't the only strange bird!) I read about this in a similar story that happened to Dutch Sheets, which he writes about it in his book, Watchman Prayer, as follows:

> *"I recall ministering in Oregon a couple years ago. My first night of speaking, I became very disoriented, confused and slightly dizzy. I wondered at first if it was a physical illness and then I began to think it*

was simply fatigue. I pushed through it, relying more heavily on my notes, and made it through the message. After the service, I began to sense the Holy Spirit, alerting me that it was witchcraft. The pastor of the church strongly agreed. Upon calling home to alert my intercessors, it was a great comfort to hear they had already discerned the attack and were covering me in prayer. Some had actually sensed it and prayed while it was happening. They smelled a rat! It never affected me again during the conference." [6]

God is alerting his people to the warfare that is being sent against them. I am so thankful that He alerts us and that He has given us the power and authority to have victory over the attack.

Preventing Backlash

I would have to say that the best way to prevent backlash is to always be on guard. Never let your guard down. We are in a war. We will see victories along the way, but we will never be at a place where we will not need to be on guard and ready to fight. Ephesians 6:10-18 says:

"Finally, my brethren, be strong in the Lord and in the power of His might. Put on the whole armor of God that you may be able to stand against the wiles of the devil. For we do not wrestle against flesh and blood, but against principalities, against powers, against the rulers of the darkness of this age, against spiritual hosts of wickedness in the heavenly places. Therefore take up the whole armor of God, that you may be able to withstand in the evil day and having done all, to stand. Stand therefore, having girded your waist with truth, having put on the breastplate of righteousness, and having shod your feet with the preparation of the gospel of peace; above all, taking the shield of faith with which you will be able to

quench all the fiery darts of the wicked one. And take
the helmet of salvation, and the sword of the Spirit,
which is the word of God; praying always with all
prayer and supplication in the Spirit, being watchful
to this end with all perseverance and supplication for
all the saints."

This scripture gives us great advice for the war we are in. First of all, if we are going to battle we must have on the whole armor of God to enable us to fight against the powers that come against us. Along with having our armor in place we must persevere in prayer, praying always with all prayer and supplication in the Spirit. And most importantly, we are exhorted to be **watchful to the end.** If we will stay equipped in our armor, pray continuously and stay watchful, we will find that our victories become more than our defeats.

Barbara Wentroble gives some principles for preventing backlash in her book *"Prophetic Intercession,"* a portion of which are as follows:

"As a result of seeking the Lord for strategy to prevent
backlash from the enemy, several principles have
emerged.

- *Faithful Follow-up – The first principle for*
  preventing backlash is to be faithful in follow-up
  prayer. Many times we engage in powerful times of
  intercession before a major event. Once the event
  is over and the victory is won, we let down in our
  prayer life. The necessity for intense prayer just
  doesn't seem necessary. However, that is usually
  the time we need to pray the most.

- *Step-by-Step Inquiry – Another principle in*
  preventing backlash is to inquire of the Lord each
  step of the way. Although David had sought the
  Lord for victory in the past, he also inquired of the
  Lord with each new step he took. The strategy for

one battle may not be the strategy for the next battle.

- **Guard Your Heart** – *A third principle in preventing backlash is to guard the heart. After a hard battle, it is easy to let anger, bitterness or even pride get in.*

- **Maintain Connections** – *A fourth principle in preventing backlash is to maintain God's chosen connections in our lives. When we are joined with other believers, there is an exponential increase in power. Isolation leaves a person vulnerable to further attacks from the enemy. The Bible calls the Church an army. An army does not consist of a single soldier, but of many soldiers joined together.*

- **Spiritual Accountability** – *A final principle to prevent backlash is to be sure that you are accountable to spiritual authority. Accountability is not a place of bondage but a place of freedom. Too often I find intercessors without proper spiritual protection. These intercessors are vulnerable to spiritual attacks, deception and many fiery darts of the enemy.* [7]

These are excellent principles for us to follow in order to help prevent backlash. I believe if we will incorporate these principles, along with stationing our watchmen upon the walls, we will begin to find that we will be able to diminish much of the backlash. We will most likely see less wounded soldiers and more victories in the Spirit!

---

[1] Rick Joyner, *Overcoming Witchcraft* (Charlotte, NC: MorningStar Publications, 1996,1997), p. 7. Used by permission. www.morningstarminstries.org

[2] Joyner, *Overcoming Witchcraft*, p. 14.

[3] Joyner, *Overcoming Witchcraft*, pp. 22-23.

[4] Joyner, *Overcoming Witchcraft*, p. 22

[5] Joyner, *Overcoming Witchcraft*, p. 24-27

[6] Dutch Sheets, *Watchman Prayer* (Ventura, CA: Regal Books, 2000), p. 70.

[7] Barbara Wentroble, *Prophetic Intercession* (Ventura, CA: Renew Books, 1999), pp.170-175.

THE BESTSELLING:

Parables in the Night Seasons; Understanding Your Dreams

By
Joy Parrott

A fresh insight to the area of drams and interpretations is presented in this book. One of the ways God has been speaking to His people is in the overlooked area of dreams. God has always talked to His people in parables, and that is what dreams are…parables played out in the night season as we sleep. You will learn how you can know if your dreams are from God and some techniques to help you understand the interpretation of your dreams.

Joy Parrott

ISBN 0-9727720-0-6

Glory Publications
35855 57th Ave. So.
Auburn, WA 98001
(253) 288-0574
www.joyparrott.com

If you would like more information
on additional materials
or would like to schedule
a ministry engagement

Please Contact:

Joy Parrott Ministries
35855 57th Ave. So.
Auburn, WA 98001
(253) 288-0574

www.joyparrott.com
Hisjoy@integrity.com

Please inquire about quantity discounts